LARRY O'BRIEN
ETHICAL ENTREPRENEURSHIP

A GUIDE TO **SURVIVING** THE COMING ECONOMIC CRISIS

...short, clear and a compelling read for anyone considering starting their own company.

Brian McGarry,
CEO of Hulse, Playfair and
McGarry Funeral Homes

FRE3DOM PRESS
CANADA INC.

Ethical Entrepreneurship:
A Guide to Surviving the Coming Economic Crisis

Freedom Press Canada Inc
12-111 Fourth Ave. , Suite 185
St. Catharines, ON L2S 3P5

Printed in the United States of America

ISBN: 978-1-9276840-1-6

LARRY O'BRIEN
ETHICAL ENTREPRENEURSHIP

A GUIDE TO
SURVIVING
THE COMING
ECONOMIC
CRISIS

Jessica

love you!

"*...short, clear and a compelling read for anyone considering starting their own company.*"

Brian McGarry,
CEO of Hulse, Playfair and
McGarry Funeral Homes

FRE3DOM PRESS
CANADA INC.

Endorsements

"Larry O'Brien is practical, crisp, thoughtful, realistic and entertaining. His book is a very compelling personal memoir for anyone contemplating being an entrepreneur."

• *Anthony Griffiths Chairman of Russel Metals Inc. and Novadaq Technologies Inc. formerly a member of the Board of Calian Technologies and the author of Corporate Catalyst*

"Many CEOs have written books about their experiences ... only one ... has been written by a CEO who grew up struggling to overcome an undiagnosed learning disability in the 1950s, launched a business in the early 1980s that currently generates annual revenues of $220 million, and then became the mayor of a country's capital. That CEO is Larry O'Brien. The lessons and insights he shares are moving, succinct, valuable and motivating. The tools are essential for anyone serious about success in hard times."

• *Tony Bailetti Ph. D. Director, Technology Innovation Management Program Carleton University, Chair of the Lead to Win Council, Ottawa, Ontario, Canada*

"I am very proud of both the high ethical standards and the professional culture enjoyed by Calian today and also the fact that their roots can be traced back to the humble beginnings when Larry founded the company. There is no doubt that these attributes, which were developed during the formative stages, played an important role in Calian's 30-year journey of growth and prosperity."

• *Ray Basler C. A. President and CEO of Calian Technologies*

"Short, clear and a compelling read for anyone considering starting their own company."

• *Brian McGarry, CEO of Hulse, Playfair and McGarry Funeral Homes. He received the Order of Ottawa in 1994 for economic development*

"I invested in Larry's first company and watched it fail in six short months. As I watched the growth of his second company Calian Technologies, it was like a new man had been born with values and ethics that did not exist in his first venture. Calian soared with success. This book is a summary of his lessons learned from failure and it is worth the read by anyone considering starting their own business. There is no substitute for experience."

• *Gerry McGee, angel investor*

"This book is dedicated to the many
people who helped make Calian Technologies Ltd.
into the ethical and successful company it is today."

Larry O'Brien, Founder

Acknowledgements

I have been blessed by God with the love and support of many people on the path to success and for that I am truly thankful to the Lord. With His help, I was lifted out of depression and gained the strength to study why I failed; then He guided me to success in the start-up and growth of Calian Technologies Ltd.

My success with Calian would not have been possible if I had not learned lessons from the failure of my first company—Insta-Call. I would like to thank Merv Sullivan and his wife Jessica for giving me refuge after that failure and being wonderful role models for me to look up to. I spent the next 28 months studying the failure, resolving problems and absorbing the lessons of the failure. Working for Merv and Jessica graciously set the stage for Calian's ethical success and for that I owe them a debt of gratitude.

It would be remiss of me not to point out people like Norris Pettis, who in the early days of my new business came up with the name Calian at his cottage at Lake Calabogie. "Curly" helped me register the company and guided me as I took the second plunge into business. Then there was that wonderful friend Kim Clohessy who, besides being a gifted Engineer, organized my first contract between his company Dy-4 Systems and Calian. And, of course, Don Armstrong who was my landlord, mentor and an investor in Calian in the very early days. They are all with the Lord now, but I know they understand how appreciative I was for their help.

Shortly after starting Calian, I was introduced to Ed Lambert, who was essential to the maintenance of the ethics and success we started to enjoy in the early days. He always won the big projects that put Calian on the firm financial ground we needed in the beginning. The first accountant I had in 1982 was Tom Coates and he came back to run a large part of the company five years later. Without these two ethical and professional supporters Calian would never have continued on the path to success.

Family is important on everyone's journey, and I was certainly blessed with support. My key business advisor was my then father-in-law, Don Green. A wise and accomplished industrialist, he was never too busy to give me insights. One of the proudest moments I had was when he looked at my balance sheet one year and said, "Calian is a serious company now—good work". Between him and his daughter, my then wife Debbie, they never let me be satisfied with taking the easy way out of any situation. They always reminded me of the moral high ground I was committed to taking and keeping. My former wife was always there in the early days, editing papers one day and entertaining clients at our home the next. Thank you Debbie.

The turning point at Calian was the acquisition of SED Systems in Saskatoon in 1990, a company three times our size at the time. It definitely would not have succeededwithout the help of my lawyer Jim Curran and his good friend Cy McDonald. They worked on the political side of the transaction while Dugald Buchanan and Ray Basler toiled away on details. I owe them a debt of gratitude as they worked hard to make Calian into a world class organization. I know I have missed many individuals and I apologize for that, but I acknowledge all of you in your roles in helping define the lessons shared in this book.

This book would not be possible without the support of my wife Colleen. I have often said I married the nicest person I have ever met and that realization continues to inspire me each day I wake up. Lastly, I thank my editor Jonathan Schmidt and my publisher Tristan Emmanuel, who guided me through the process of writing this guide book. They were patient and accommodating as I learned the ropes of writing my first book on ethics. Thank you.

FREEDOM PRESS
CANADA INC.

For more information on other books published
by Freedom Press Canada Inc. see:

www. freedompress. ca

For more information about Larry O'Brien
and Ethical Entrepreneurship see:

www. facebook. com/ethicalentrepreneurship

Contents

Foreword

Many CEOs have written books about their experiences. However, only one of these books has been written by a CEO who grew up struggling to overcome an undiagnosed learning disability in the 1950s, launched a business in the early 1980s that currently generates annual revenues of $220 million, and then became the mayor of a country's capital city in 2006. That CEO is Larry O'Brien.

This book is an enjoyable read, concise, to the point, and embodies Larry's belief in what it takes to become successful. The lessons and insights he shares are moving, succinct, valuable and motivating. The tools are useful.

Larry's book is more about achieving success through a drive to emancipate vs. combining resources to profitably satisfy customers. Larry writes in a clear and concise manner to outline and describe the many insights and lessons learned throughout his very interesting career. He speaks from the heart to individuals who wish to be successful.

Larry grew up in a family that experienced financial problems and he himself encountered financial difficulties at the beginning of his professional career, including bankruptcy. This book describes the lessons Larry learned while he worked hard to move away from a situation that was not acceptable to him. He eventually became wealthy and self-sufficient. Then he turned politician.

The lessons and insights Larry gained while moving from bankruptcy to successful entrepreneur to politician are valuable. Readers will find each chapter inspiring and meaningful.

I feel compelled to describe how Larry's book fits with what we know about entrepreneurs. Entrepreneurship is at the core of prosperity and can be examined at the individual, company, city and country levels. Entrepreneurship at the individual level can be best conceptualized as being a two-sided coin. One side of the entrepreneurship coin focuses on what individuals do to identify and exploit opportunities. This approach has been applied for hundreds of years. To date, economists have contributed most of the knowledge about entrepreneurship we teach students. Most economists explain what entrepreneurs do in terms of combining resources and processes to profitably deliver value to their customers. From economists we learned the differences that exist between the disruptive entrepreneur and the alert entrepreneur.

The second side of the entrepreneurship coin focuses on what entrepreneurs do to emancipate, or move away from a present state or replace/destroy it. The study of entrepreneurship using an emancipation lens is relatively new. While the study of entrepreneurship as a drive to emancipate is interdisciplinary, it is currently led by academics who study social life, social change, as well as the social causes and consequences of human behavior.

Larry's book fits naturally with the second side of the coin. It provides many lessons that can be organized around three attributes of emancipation: (1) the need to seek autonomy; (2) the need to author relationships; and (3) the need to make declarations.

Readers will find Larry's view essential in learning what is needed to become successful in terms of an individual's drive to emancipate.

In closing, I would like to acknowledge Larry's many contributions to Canada's Capital Region before, during and after he was the mayor of the city of Ottawa. While Larry was mayor, Lead to Win was re-launched as a job creation engine fuelled by technology entrepreneurs; also, an online journal, known today as the TIM Review, was launched to benefit technology and global entrepreneurs. Larry continues to be a strong supporter of entrepreneurship in the region.

Read on!

Tony Bailetti Ph. D.
Director, Technology Innovation Management Program
Carleton University
Chair of the Lead to Win Council, Ottawa, Ontario, Canada

Prologue

Another Business Book? Really?

Trust me. I know. The last thing the world needs is another business book from some egomaniacal CEO who thinks he knows how the world should be run. I've even read some of them. Not bad. Lots of smart folks and lots of great advice.

So what does Larry O'Brien have to say that hasn't been said before?

It was my intent that the first book I wrote after leaving politics would be about the life of an entrepreneur who became a politician. The stories of the cast of characters and political shenanigans that took place during my term as the 58th Mayor of Ottawa will be even more humorous as the toasts are being sipped to celebrate the first kick off of the new Ottawa CFL football team and the first subway passenger takes the down ride on the escalator to enjoy the world class transportation system that will be in place in 2017.

So I have decided to write a book to help some people become self-sufficient under any economic circumstances. I believe that the prosperity of Canada is dependent upon the success of entrepreneurs who build strong companies that create jobs and wealth for our Citizens. I think it is critical that we encourage the men and women of our country to acquire the skills needed to build a company that could last forever.

But there is a much better—a much more fundamental reason—why I think I might actually have something worthwhile to say. It's this: I have made most—if not all—of the mistakes you can possibly make starting a company.

And even a few mistakes that are almost impossible to make.

The questions I hope to help you answer include:

- how to build the passion to succeed
- how to choose the right business for you
- how to make good choices
- how to build the business
- how to hire
- when to say "no"
- lessons learned along the way

So if you have ever thought to yourself "I'd like to start my own business but I'm afraid of losing my shirt," read on. I'll tell you something: I lost a heck of a lot more than my shirt. And if I can learn from my failures and come back to start a successful business, you can too.

Why You Should Read This Book

Change is mandatory; progress is optional

I have spent much of my waking hours over the last few years trying to evaluate our economy and what the future looks like. I have been a politician and I have been a successful entrepreneur. I believe strongly that the lifeboat for many in our society over the next ten years will be selecting, starting and then building a business that will provide security for themselves and their families over the troubling political and economic times ahead.

My goal is not to alarm the reader or induce a sense of doom and gloom. Quite the opposite, in fact. The last thing we need is yet another "expert" pessimist raining down more evidence of imminent catastrophe. As I have said, "I've never met a rich pessimist." What I hope I can do is to simply remind you that the economy is not a reliable and smoothly functioning machine whose results are easily and consistently predictable. It only looks that way because we tend to get comfortable with what works; it's when things go pear-shaped that we suddenly pull our heads from out of the sand and wonder, what the heck is happening?

A nice metaphor for what is happening is, believe it or not, the tragedy of the *Titanic*. The *Titanic* was billed as the greatest and the safest ocean liner ever built. And yet in her maiden voyage in 1912 she collided with an iceberg in the dark and more than fifteen hundred people died. And why? A combination of design flaws, poor planning, human error and hubris—a hubris that made it impossible for anyone to believe that a ship so technically advanced could fail. Or to put it in a contemporary vernacular: too big to fail.

Sound familiar?

Most of us can't even consider the possibility that our way of life could change dramatically over the next decade. After all, life is still amazing here in North America and many of us feel safe—after all if it was going to get bad anytime soon wouldn't our duly elected political leaders warn us? The answer to that question is simple: in our democracy we have a tendency to shoot the messenger and that makes telling the difficult news very hard.

Consider for a minute what must have been the terrible confusion among officers on board the *Titanic*. This can't be happening, must have been the first reaction. This can't be happening.

Think back to the economic crisis that unhinged the global markets in 2008. The verdict of conventional wisdom—the status quo—was that the Fed and Treasury were perceived as "unsinkable." It's an illusion that has cost trillions of dollars—trillions of dollars of new debt that now burden the taxpayers: $2 trillion added to the Fed balance sheet, $1. 2 trillion in secret giveaways to the banking cartel, and $6 trillion in additional Federal debt/spending.

Our reaction was, this can't be happening.

But it was.

And it still is.

Challenges we face

There is a massive global sovereign debt crisis that will; (a) make it impossible for countries to pay existing social benefits by 2020; (b) cause the destruction of the global banking system, and; (c) cause the US currency to lose its status as the world reserve currency.

The above will result in serious deterioration of the European economies—inevitably followed by the United States and Canada. Housing deflation coupled with commodity hyperinflation will badly hurt the middle class in North America and create shortages in food, fuel and the basic needs of the population.

This economic hardship will lead to substantial domestic social unrest. Talking about the current economy, watching what is going on, I often think, is this what some Europeans were thinking just before 1939? Why do we think we are immune from gigantic social upheavals?

Normalcy bias in action

The fact is, very few of us are willing to voluntarily abandon a belief system that supports the status quo. It's called the normalcy bias. Remember that old chestnut from Galileo about a body in motion wanting to stay in motion? Same thing. How we think about things is a habit that is hard to break. We are like those passengers on the *Titanic* ten minutes after its fatal encounter with the iceberg: we can't believe such a grand ship could sink. The result?

Instead of using the time we have to react and respond and stabilize our situation, we do nothing. And hope the ship will re-float itself on its own.

Some of our reluctance can be attributed to a kind of algorithm of disbelief: the gap grows between what we know is inevitable (the ship will sink) and what we see (the damage to the hull doesn't appear that serious). If this gap grows too wide, the sense is that we have no control over our fate.

I am here to tell you, however, that you do have control over your fate. You always have and you always will. The problem comes back to perception: if you think along with the talking heads of conventional wisdom that there is no danger—and that even if there was some danger there are more than enough lifeboats on board—then you will sink with everyone else.

I don't want that to happen.

The financial system of the United States of America is like the *Titanic*. Hubris led many to declare it financially unsinkable even as its fundamental design was riddled with fatal flaws and the human pilots in charge ran it straight into the iceberg at top speed.

Passengers who believed the publicized fiction that the *Titanic* was unsinkable had less than three hours to come to terms with the horrifying deceit of that claim.

We have a little more time. But that begs the obvious question: if conventional wisdom tells you that the system is too big to fail, and fails anyway, how confident are you that the same conventional wisdom is not trying to tell you what needs to be done to fix the system?

The story of the *Titanic* is normalcy bias in action—or non-action, if you like. How could so many intelligent people not try to save themselves? It is the "this can't happen here" mentality that prevents action in the face of certain danger.

The mathematically inevitable collapse of the dollar will change our paradigm forever—and rest assured, it will collapse. The writing has been on the wall for a long time. The iceberg is long in our rearview, but we are taking on water. Not to fear; I can still hear the orchestra playing!

Consider:

- Record debt by nations will destroy the banking system and force hyperinflation
- Social programs can't be paid and that will incite riots
- 401K holders will start pulling money out of the market
- Peak oil will ruin the economy
- Political unrest (Islamists, anarchists, communists, revolutionaries)
- USD will lose reserve Standard—China and Russia selling USD

These risks will add up and in one or a number of ways work to increase unemployment and increase inflation, making life difficult for anyone counting on the current economy to remain constant. It will change.

Is this scary stuff? No doubt about it. And I expect a skeptical response. How could things really be as bad as O'Brien says? Isn't he just trying to capitalize on people's fears and anxieties about the economy? Surely, things will get much better. There is no reason to worry.

Okay. Fair enough. But do me a favour. It's a thought experiment. Before you dismiss my assessment out of hand, take a few minutes to think about those passengers on the deck of the *Titanic*. Imagine yourself just minutes before the alarm was sounded. An officer walks towards you. You ask him about the alarm. And what do you think he would say?

"There is no cause for alarm. Trust me."

I repeat: change is mandatory; progress is optional.

I say it is time to consider starting your own business, and let me tell you how. Nothing is too big to fail. But using the principles outlined here as a foundation for your business will sustain you and your business in good times and bad. You will be able to provide security for yourself and your family.

And that is the best security there is.

How You Should Read This Book

This isn't a long book. But it has taken a lifetime to write.

The really important lessons in life are like that.

Some of the book is serious in tone and some of it is more humorous.

Occasionally I have distilled into a sentence or two what took me months—sometimes years—to learn. And because my life is the only story I really know from the beginning, I have included anecdotes—some long and some short—that I hope will help flesh out the tips, rules and principals outlined.

The reason for writing at length about myself is not ego; I am not the kind of person who needs to hear himself. It is much simpler and more practical than that: I have really only learned by doing.

It is my hope that you don't read this book with the idea that you will learn some secret that will allow you to bypass or short-circuit all the passion, hard work and commitment it takes to succeed. Let's get that straight right from the beginning: there is no magic key to the fairy kingdom. So if that is what you are after, stop reading right now.

Here is another important point: I don't think that what it takes to be a success in business is any different from what it takes to be a good human being. In fact, they are identical. We are all connected. There is no escaping our obligations. So a huge part of my approach—its essence—will be a focus on (get ready!) ... ethics.

You read that right.

Ethics: values, virtues, principles, character and so on. As I have said to people many times, business is not a noun; it's a verb. It isn't about what it is; it's about what you, as the business owner, do. For yourself, your employees, your customers, your community and society.

That may strike some of you as hopelessly old-fashioned. Well, guilty as charged! But here is the thing: it works. And not just in the short term. How you do business is how you live your life. Your business is what you want people to know about who you are.

So if that seems appealing to you, I invite you to read on. And remember: success is relative. I don't know how much money you want to make in your life and I don't really care. That isn't what matters. We all have our own ideas about what success means. Money comes and money goes. Our virtues are a legacy we inherit from one generation and hopefully pass on intact to another.

To me, real success is finding out about what really matters and sticking with it.

Introduction

Why Ethical?

I started my first company, Insta-Call Ltd. , in 1979. It was not an auspicious debut.

I was twenty-nine-years-old and I had the tiger by the tail. I had all the confidence in the world; my idea was solid gold. I could not fail.

Within six months I lost my entire life savings. In the blink of an eye, I lost everything. Insta-Call was an ill-conceived idea that was executed in a sloppy manner and resulted in total, absolute financial, emotional and social failure. This personal disaster left me depressed and without most of my friends and family. It left me with little hope for the future. Eventually, stress and depression took their toll on my body and I had a minor heart attack. It was a very dark and difficult time—probably the worst time in my life.

It was, however, the best thing that ever happened to me.

In 1982, twenty-eight months following the Insta-Call disaster, I started my second company. Calian Technology Ltd. was started with a total investment of $35. It began as a one-person consulting company, but by the time I retired as CEO on February 2, 2005, Calian was a publicly traded company with sales of $177 million and with profits of over $10 million. The company employed more than two thousand people. Calian grew smoothly over twenty-three years and was never in dire trouble—and not because we never confronted trouble. Business is no different from a family in that respect. You can't escape bad news. But we had the courage and the wisdom to always move forward; when we made mistakes we admitted it and recovered quickly. The key was always to get on with the job of building a company that would last forever.

We never lost our focus or our commitment to the mission. That was how it began and that is how it has stayed. So much has changed between the lines; the lines themselves, however, have never changed.

The difference between who I was with Insta-Call and who I was with Calian was like the difference between apples and oranges. So, same guy but massively different results. What happened? The difference was the plus-two years of honest and unforgiving self-reflection. I had to answer a simple question: "How could someone as smart as I thought I was screw up so badly?"

If there is one key lesson I would pass along to anyone who wants to know what it means to succeed, it would be this: to succeed you need to know what failure is. And what I mean by that is less simple than it seems. We all fail at something. I have failed so many times I have lost count. But that isn't the end of it; it's the beginning.

Few of us are as honest about ourselves as we need to be. The point is not to beat yourself up and embrace defeatism. The idea is to be honest about what it was that caused you to fail and to figure out what you need to do instead to succeed. It isn't enough risking everything you own. Sometimes you have to risk everything you are. So, who are you?

I believe I found the answer to that question, and within that answer lies some of the secrets of success for any person trying to make a difference in the world.

As the old saying goes, "I have been down and I have been up and up is definitely better." My success in business has enabled me to help raise two children, create thousands of jobs, meet fabulous people, shake hands with several US presidents, dine with prime ministers, travel as an official state visitor of Canada, play golf at Augusta, almost buy the Ottawa Rough Riders, be blessed by the Dali Lama and then be elected the fifty-eighth mayor of Ottawa.

As I said, it has taken me a lifetime in business—and too many failures to count—to learn what I know. But if I had to condense an entire life into ten points, this would be the list.

You may have your own ideas. At first, though, I would try and unlearn everything you think you know and memorize my list. These principles have been my personal mantra from the very beginning and I have never wavered in my commitment to them. I guarantee that if you stick to them, they will work for you too. And don't worry, each will be discussed later in this book and in more detail.

1) You can make money in two ways: doing something no one else can do or doing something no one else wants to do.

2) The perfect business success is a combination of the Space Cadet and the Street Fighter. The tricky part is getting the mix right and over time.

3) The four value pillars for success are: honesty, long-term thinking, adding value and prudence.

4) Never buy your banker lunch.

5) Give your customer 10 percent more than he asked and charge him 10 percent less than he expects.

6) Never hire anyone who will not admit to a mistake.

7) Business is a verb, not a noun. You make money from what you do, not from what you know.

8) Never let your goals be your limitations.

9) Never bite off anything bigger than your head.

10) When the horse dies, dismount.

I wanted the word "ethical" in the title for a very specific reason: it is important. It is important to me for reasons that you will discover in the course of reading this book. Does an ethical approach to business have to be meaningful to you? Do you need ethics to succeed?

No. You do not. And if an ethical approach to success is not your thing, I would recommend you stop reading right now. This book is not for you.

Then what is my point? Just this: I do not recognize and never will recognize any difference between the businessperson and the human being. What I do in business is how I want to treat my fellow human beings and how I want to be treated in turn. We are not alone on this planet. We have obligations to each other.

Financial success is wonderful. Happiness is even better.

Chapter One

Getting Started and Staying in the Game: the Four Value Rules are All You Need to Know

I was 13 when I became a paperboy for the *Ottawa Journal*. It was my very first entrepreneurial experience.

The way I figured it, five dollars every two weeks meant that I could walk to a local restaurant after school and buy a chocolate milkshake with real ice cream for a quarter or a full club sandwich with French fries and a coke for $1.25.

In 1962 there were two fierce rivals in the newspaper business in Ottawa: the *Journal* and the *Citizen*. My competition, the *Citizen*, eventually put the *Journal* out of business in 1980. But they never conquered my route. It's a fact that still makes me smile with pride.

First lesson: never underestimate any achievement no matter how small. Success has a lot to do with the right habits and the right frame of mind. Passion, right? Commitment? Following through on a job no matter what?

It was my goal, for instance, to have every house on my route take the *Journal*. It wasn't enough to have 50 percent or 65 percent. I wanted the 100 percent. That was my mission. Interestingly, the pocket money I earned—while important (it got me into the paperboy business in the first place!)—was not as important overall as the goal I had created for myself. Money is not—and never can be—a mission.

I learnt a lot about business and marketing from this paper route.

My route had sixty homes. Starting out I had forty daily papers to deliver every night after school and five or six Saturday-only papers. I figured out that there were about ten more homes that likely could be persuaded to take the *Journal* and I made it my personal goal to see and to convert them. I delivered free papers as often as I could and often knocked on doors to talk up the value of the *Journal* over the *Citizen*. I was relentless.

Was it my adolescent charm and salesmanship? Or was it the simple fact that converting to the *Journal* was the easiest way of getting rid of me? Either way, eventually all but three of the houses on my route converted. Selling and servicing your customers to expand your market share was an excellent lesson to learn at an early age.

The enjoyment of making money and the security it brought still affect me today. One of the clearest memories I have of that period always makes me smile. I can still see myself sitting on my bed with all of the money I collected, running my fingers through the nickels, dimes and quarters and counting and recounting the dollars. I actually took up numismatics (coin collecting) at the time just so I would have a reason to keep the money safe and not spend it.

There was a sense of security and control in feeling the nickels and dimes slip through my fingers over and over again.

Okay, a childish recollection. But what does it mean for you?

Just this: *passion*. You have to start with an idea—a venture—that is more than a something; it needs to be your *everything*.

What else?

I believe starting a company and being successful are very simple. That so many fail at starting a company is sad and it can be avoided. This entire book is dedicated to helping you avoid the mistakes I made starting my first company. It really is quite simple to be successful. Simple, yes.

But what else?

Let me explain with a recollection from a few years back.

The Banff Television Festival is the television counterpart of the Cannes Film Festival in France. Producers, network executives and financiers all converge on this tiny jewel in Alberta's Rocky Mountains once a year to mingle and search for the next big television opportunity. My company Calian was there. At the invitation and persuasion of Spar Aerospace, the leader of the Canadian Space Industry at the time, Calian was sponsoring the BTF's Rockie Award for Science and Technology. Calian had been on a substantial roll after acquiring Miller Communications and SED Systems in 1988 and 1990 respectively and we were now considered part of the Canadian technology scene. Our sales had quadrupled in 1991 to $28 million and the talk on the street was that we would soon be going public.

It felt good to enjoy some of the perks of success. My (now former) wife Debbie and my five-year-old son Michael were vacationing with me (my youngest son, Matthew, was only one and had stayed home). It was a relaxing and enjoyable time, and it was a chance meeting with greatness that crystallized my understanding of what role values had played in the success of Calian. As one of the patrons of the festival, I was invited to the sponsors' luncheon. Although I viewed this luncheon as a chore, it became a special learning opportunity. Most of the other sponsors were no-shows, and even my wife Debbie decided she was going to go shopping; it was only myself, two organizers and one other sponsor at the lunch table. To my delight, the guest of honor that year was legendary newsman Walter Cronkite! Our table also included the former festival honoree and film great Sir Peter Ustinov. I was in the company of greatness.

Walter was receiving the Award of Excellence. As in so many other households for so many years, Walter Cronkite had been a familiar and respected presence in my home every Sunday afternoon in the late fifties and sixties. I never missed an episode of his TV documentary *The 20th Century*. And of course I had been a huge fan of Peter Ustinov for years. Integrity and sincerity sang from both their voices: Sir Peter was nothing short of one of the premier actors of the century and Walter was a living legend. I was in seventh heaven until suddenly it dawned on me that my wife was going to miss out on a once-in-a-lifetime opportunity. The lunch quickly became relaxed and entertaining as these two old warhorses of the entertainment industry exchanged stories and graciously coaxed us into conversation about our own tales and experiences. The talk and the wine flowed freely and three hours passed as quickly as three minutes.

Near the end of the lunch I asked Walter about his success in broadcasting. I asked him about the values he used to build his career and his answer was very simple.

"I kept a standard of personal values that people could trust and over the years—they did trust!"

I told Walter that my wife Debbie was going to be very disappointed that she did not come to lunch today. "She has said many times how much she admires you, Mr. Cronkite."

"Her name is Debbie?" he asked.

I nodded and we parted ways. Later that afternoon when I caught up to Michael and Debbie, I recounted the stories from lunch and, as I expected,

Debbie was very disappointed. But greatness has a way of shining through the mist of disappointment.

As a sponsor, I had to go on stage that night and make the presentation of the Rockie on behalf of Calian. I escorted Debbie to our seats at the front of the main ballroom at the Banff Springs International Hotel, unaware that we had been spotted.

"You must be Debbie!"

Walter Cronkite had walked up to us with a big smile on his face. "Larry told me all about you and I am sorry we could not have lunch today."

Debbie melted in his presence.

He was both charming and down to earth and he held her hand as they chatted for a few minutes. Walter had that combination of humility and quiet confidence—a sureness of himself—that made him easily step outside the orbit of his own ego to understand my wife's disappointment. We were fans before. But now?

Second lesson: a business owner needs always to step outside the tight orbit of ego. Nothing is more important to a customer than knowing he or she is deeply appreciated and valued. This is so simple to say, but the most common error business owners commit is losing touch with the customer.

Walter Cronkite had no reason to introduce himself to my wife. What was in it for him? Nothing. But in another way, everything.

As the saying goes: Do as you would be done by.

Simple, right?

At the end of the evening, a producer of a TV documentary came up to me for a brief interview. She wanted to know a little bit about starting a small business in Canada.

"Mr. O'Brien, what was the biggest surprise you had in building Calian Technology from a one-person consulting company in 1982 until now?"

"How simple it was!" I said in a matter of fact way that I hoped did not cross the line into arrogance or overconfidence. "I was lucky enough to make all of my big mistakes three years before I started Calian and that made Calian very straightforward."

I went on to describe my models for choosing business ideas and then the four values for making rock-solid decisions swiftly. I told her why I thought most startup companies fail and why some prosper. I quickly recounted a critical few acid tests for assessing new business ideas, business models and personality traits to avoid when starting a small company. I buried her in a blizzard of ideas and thoughts about starting and building a business in Canada that could last forever. At the end of my dissertation she smiled and repeated my opening statement.

"How simple it was?" she said. She appeared doubtful.

I told her again about how important it had been to make good decisions and how I had worked eighteen hours a day for eight years to make the company succeed. I said, "It was all about building a company that would last forever."

"That sounds like very hard work!" she gasped.

I smiled at her. "I said it was simple to succeed; I never said it was easy."

The Four Rules You Need to Know About

1) Honesty
2) Long Term Thinking
3) Adding Value
4) Prudence

Simple. Easy?

Heck no! I worked my butt off for years. But it was worth it.

Always be honest

Not just honest with others but also with yourself. A businessperson must be impeccable with her word to be successful. Impeccability means without sin and that means refraining from speaking ill of others or spreading gossip. An ethically honest person will make choices that are fair to others as well as themselves and over time your business associates and friends will cheer you on to success. Honesty will also let you achieve a greater sense of reality and truth. In spirituality you have the everlasting word of God; in business you must have the bond of your word.

Remember the cliché of the handshake as a symbol of your integrity? Let me tell you something: it's true. Tell your customer what you will do and always—always—do what you say.

You must have the real facts in front of you to make a good choice. Not the hoped for or fuzzy facts, but the facts that were the result of hard work and critical thinking. Only armed with an honest approach to life and the honesty of fact can you make good business- and life choices.

One of the things that irritates me in business is the tendency to "wife swap" when it comes to business culture. What I mean is this: when you make a commitment, you stick to that commitment. Don't allow yourself to become seduced by trendy slogans or corporate consultancy mumbo jumbo. The business can change; the mission can change; the culture of your business can evolve—it must evolve. But what cannot change are the core values that structure your business. And those values have to be your personal values.

I call it my "Honest Ed" paradox. I have in my mind the stereotypical image of the slick used car dealer named Ed. You see him everywhere. His pitch—his come on to you the customer—is his honesty. Okay, when someone comes to me and the first thing he says is how honest he is, my first thought is, no you aren't. Not if you have to tell me that! Run like heck!

When is the last time you believed a politician who tried to come across as just another working class stiff or "one of the guys."

Honesty is not what you do or say. It is who you are. Honesty requires you to deal with the truth in every situation. This is not as easy at seems since the truth can hide behind the clutter and noise of life and business. You need the truth, not the "hoped for" truth, not the "article of faith" truth, but rather the detailed, hard, indisputable facts that can't be argued with. This requires a tremendous amount of hard work and it can be tough to make an honest assessment of any situation you are in.

Another thing about honesty: it is easy to remember. The honest person always has the truth at his disposal. Remember honesty is your best competitive advantage.

Never promise more than you are prepared to deliver.

Always admit a mistake. Remember, it isn't the mistake that matters; we all make mistakes. It's how you fix it that matters to your customer.

Always think long-term

You're never going to get to your destination—your goal—by staring at your feet.

Sounds obvious, but it is truly instructive to take note of how often we allow ourselves to lose touch with the goals we have created for ourselves and end up walking in circles and forgetting why we're here. Another way to think of strategic long-term thinking is this: don't make a meal out of the hors d'oeuvres!

Amazing and hard to believe, but true: the long-term solution often produces the most positive short-term results.

How?

First, problem solving is a complex skill that can only be learned with experience. What I have learned is that inexperience tends to produce a panic that that is easily alleviated by seizing on the most obvious solution. Sort of like being hungry and grabbing at the lowest-hanging apple you see on the tree. It's in reach, so you grab it.

Never let panic steer you to a solution. Panic is your backseat driver. Always take the time to stand back and try to find some distance and objectivity. Think: this solution will solve my short-term problem, but what then?

If the answer to that question is anything like "I'm not sure" then you have a problem. And be wary of so-called experts offering "quick fixes."

What other benefits are there to long-term thinking?

It puts you and your business alongside other businesses that are thinking long-term; they, in turn, will help you along to success. If you're pushing a rock uphill and so is someone else, doesn't it make sense for both of you to push the same rock? It is called "factor X" (we will be talking about it more later) and you can never foresee the help that will come to you until you make the right long-term choice. It's tough to make long-term decisions when you are fixated on short-term solutions. The point is, you can't ask a sprinter to run a marathon. Short-term solutions are tempting for a simple reason: they are usually readily available. But as a business owner you need to be always focused on the horizon. It doesn't mean short-term problems can be ignored. Part of being a successful business owner means taking action and being decisive.

The key is consistency. Long-term thinking is by necessity consistent; it becomes collaborative. Even better, it can be learned and put in practice by people who work for you. You want employees who are innovative and resourceful. But you need to be focused on the mission. The best way to do that is by thinking long-term. It helps them become invested in the mission—and it doesn't take an Einstein to figure out that people will work harder for you if they believe they have a stake in the outcome.

Short-term thinking is episodic and "one time only."

Have you noticed how people who are obsessed with a problem tend to look down at the ground and in general are not aware of what is going on around them? The best answer to any short-term problem is always inherent in the long-term solution. I use the twenty-year rule; if I think I might remember the choice in twenty years it had better be the right choice.

Always add value to anything you do

Business is a verb, not a noun; you should only make money for what you do and not what you know. If you know something that will help another, it is usury to charge them for that knowledge unless you are adding value as well.

This insight will pay back dividends from others as your reputation grows. It can be your choice: earn a reputation as a user or be awarded the reputation as an outstanding and generous businessperson.

Another handy way to remember this rule—and more important to implement the rule—is always to give your customers 10 percent more than they expect and charge them 10 percent less than agreed to. Loyalty is a value. One of the best. If as a business owner you are always thinking about how you can improve the value of what you are providing your customer, you are always reinforcing your customer's loyalty.

Business is a long-term proposition. Whatever it is you are producing, whatever service you are providing, you want the perception from your customer to be that your customer's business is valued. It is always more expensive to acquire new customers than it is to hold onto the customers you already have. Adding value is key. This is just as true with how you treat the people you work with. You want people to enjoy working with you, even want to work with you because they know that they will be rewarded for their efforts. It can be your choice: earn a reputation as a user or abuser or be rewarded with the reputation of a business owner who is an outstanding, fair and just person.

Always be prudent

We all know what prudent means: exercising good judgment, being shrewd, discreet and circumspect in decisions or advice. Think of prudence as the internal gyro that keeps you and your business upright and stable.

To me, there is a subtle but profound difference between prudence and caution. The one is positive; the other is negative. What do I mean?

Starting a business is scary enough. When it comes to starting your own business, if you need too much outside help, you can assume you do not know enough about the business to succeed. The prudent approach would be to break the business model down into its components and study them and figure out how it will work. Decide what you need to know. Prudence tells you what feels right and what doesn't. If you develop prudent habits you will always be secure in whatever decision you make. That doesn't necessarily mean the decision will be the right one! Sound inconsistent? Not at all. No system is 100 percent failure-proof. But prudence is the most reliable tool you will ever come across to maximize your odds.

I have made many decisions in my career that have not worked out as planned. However, over the years and with experience I realized something interesting: I wasn't making bad decisions. Right or wrong? Sure. But that's inevitable. What is avoidable is making bad decisions. In fact, almost all the bad decisions I have ever made in my life have come down to the same reason: imprudence.

Prudence is a positive value because it becomes who you are. Caution, on the other hand, is negative because it can be a sign of who you aren't. It's a measure of what you are either unwilling to do or afraid of doing. You—the business owner—need to be able to make decisions. Not tomorrow or next week … *now*. The cautious person tends to delay decisions because he is always waiting for that one missing piece of information that will somehow resolve the equation.

It may not be obvious early on in your career, but something that you will come to realize is that protecting your resources is critical; the waste of resources has been the ruin of many businesses. By resources I do not mean only capital. You are your greatest resource! Your emotional and physical assets are a resource. As we have touched upon already, you and your business—especially at the beginning—are one and the same thing. How you relate to your customer is how that customer will relate to your business. Nothing is more valuable to a small business owner than his good name and reputation. Practicing prudence will allow you to protect the gains you have made and enhance your reputation.

The four values—call them O'Brien's Laws—outlined here are fundamental to building a company that will last forever. I know, because I have achieved the results that prove it. The first three laws—combined with commitment and hard work—will enable you to start and build a business. The fourth law will help ensure that you keep what you worked so hard to earn.

I am going to make a big promise to you: using these four rules will work for you. But as the TV commercials remind you: certain conditions may apply.

First: you need to be fully committed. It isn't a system that can be applied periodically or cherry-picked. It's like pretending you can be "sort of pregnant": either you are or you aren't. Are you in? or are you out? No "maybes" or "for the most part."

Second: you need a set of core values.

Three: your business—your mission—must be aligned and in synch with those basic core values. Not just at the beginning, but all the way to the end.

Practice makes perfect

The more you use the rules the better they will work. There is also a wonderful cumulative effect that gathers in your wake as you use the rules to steer through the obstacles on your way to success. The more you use them, the more people seeing you use them, the more people that trust you will use the rules the more powerful they become.

If I had asked those questions in 1979 when I was thinking about Insta-Call I would never have started the company.

Lesson learned!

Chapter Two

Failure is the Best Teacher You Will Ever Have

Someone once told me I had earned a street MBA, and they were right. So what is the big difference between an academic MBA and the street MBA? The latter can only be learned—*earned*—on the way down. And for me, that has made all the difference. But after that, everything was on the way up.

I touched briefly already on my Insta-Call experience, but let's take a closer look. In reading about my first real business venture, I want you to think about yours.

The failure of Insta-Call was the nadir of my life; surprisingly, it was also the highlight of my life.

I was twenty-nine years old and I had what I believed was a can't-lose idea that would make millions. I had two other things: pride and a cocky confidence. As it turned out, what I actually had was an over-active imagination and very little common sense and what turned out to be just about the dumbest idea ever.

In 1979, unlike today, the radio frequencies that cell phones and pagers worked on were different in every city in Canada, and for that matter, almost every city in the US. This meant that it was impossible to roam freely with the same cell phone or radio pager. I had a world-beating solution to the lack of roaming service for pagers. I was going to start a nationwide radio-paging company and become very rich.

I took what money I had and bought a bunch of pagers. I also invested in a beautifully designed kiosk that I was sure could be installed at every airport, every train station and every bus station in Canada to provide radio pagers and cell phones to traveling business people. My traveling customers could pick up and hand in pagers and cell phones at their leisure for a single low rate of $4. 50 per day.

Man, I thought to myself, I am a genius!

My very first booth—the start of a communications empire—was at the Ottawa International Airport.

To say I was confident of my prospects is an understatement. I was so confident I was already thinking about what colour my flashy new Mercedes was going to be. My only worry was, leather interior or not? I went into the pager venture asking, "How can I lose?" That I had no business experience and I did not have any facts to support my belief did not dampen my enthusiasm.

My idea was a slam-dunk. I had pitched the pager concept to several companies and corporations, and I was amazed at the positive responses. Who wouldn't be interested in being able to track down staff members anywhere in the country on a moment's notice? But did I nail down any corporate contracts? Not a one. I figured I didn't need one. They would come around before too long. It was only a matter of time.

I stood in that airport booth day-in and day-out for almost six months. And in that entire time I did not rent a single pager. Not to anyone—not even a friend.

The fantasy of a blue Mercedes with creamy leather interior gave way to a nightmare quickly taking shape: I was running out of money. My first business—my can't-lose idea—was failing.

The "how can I lose?" question slowly changed to "what was I thinking?"

The end was mercifully short.

I said that no one rented a pager. That was not actually true. I rented one.

An executive walked up to my booth one afternoon and asked to rent a pager. My dreams were coming true! I was in business! I was back on track for the blue Mercedes. Why stop there? Why not toss in a huge and spacious lake-front cottage!

As he walked away with my $300 pager I held the $4. 50 rental fee tightly in my hand thinking about the 40 percent gross margin I was making. I had worked the math this way and that. I believed with my first rental the avalanche of success would start. I was in a dreamland of blissful contentment until the next day when I asked, "Where did that pager go?"

My first and only customer stole the pager! I never saw him or that pager again and Insta-Call was closed within a few days. It was over and I was crushed.

I had lost all my money. I was forced to declare bankruptcy, and not the relatively gentle corporate version of bankruptcy either. This was the brutal, messy, unsentimental kick-in-the-face version of insolvency that destroys your optimism and craters your hope.

My self-esteem was in the toilet. My car was towed, my condo apartment was foreclosed and my wages were garnished. I ended up in ICU at the Queensway Carleton Hospital in Ottawa listening to a young doctor expressing concern about the punishing lifestyle that had resulted in an "interesting" heartbeat for a twenty-nine-year-old jogger.

I entered what I now call the post-mortem phase of my business apprenticeship. I had hit bottom. But despite all the humiliation and anguish and pain, I realized I still had a desire to be a success. So, in the dark depths of bankruptcy and shame—armed with nothing so much as a major dose of newfound humility—I set about rebuilding the base of my value system. In many ways, I was a very lucky man. I still had that deep drive to succeed; but I realized that the most formidable obstacle to achieving that goal was my own pride. My abject failure had shamed that pride into nonexistence.

I had earned my first street MBA! You learn on the way down and you earn on the way back up.

The postmortem questions were chilling. Did I ask the wrong questions of the wrong people? Should I have been asking the travelers, "When you are traveling would you like to be contacted on a minute's notice by your boss?" The answers, I suspect, would not have been encouraging. As a smart technologist, why did I not think about the long-term solution to the problem of roaming? What I had come up with was—at best—a short-term option. Dumb!

Instead of investing in building up the wireless network with common frequencies and more antenna towers—long-term thinking—I had foolishly invested in a wooden kiosk where for six months I could practice standing for increasingly extended periods of time doing nothing but gazing at my navel.

Before launching that first "business," I had hired some so-called consultants to fine-tune my enterprise. At the time they were enthusiastic and had voted a big thumbs-up. Another lesson! Where were they now? Nowhere. The problem with a consultant is that you want honesty but what you are buying is enthusiasm. Why had I asked a consultant to provide for pay what a random sampling of potential customers—i. e. random business travelers at the airport—could have told me for free. And who was going to pay for that Mercedes—consultants? or customers?

I had nothing but questions that mostly all started with the words "why" or "how come." The answers all pointed back to me.

I realized too late that I knew absolutely nothing about the pager business. Had I approached an existing pager company and tried to sell them on the idea of opening up booths across the country, I would have received a polite "no". Years later, whenever asked for my advice on a new business venture that was going to rock a specific industry, I would often ask if the promoter had tried to sell the idea to companies in the specific industry they were about to revolutionize.

Another lesson: usually you don't know nearly as much as you think you do. Knowing that will help you find the information you do need. Remember: you don't need to know everything, but you need to know enough to know what you don't know. In my case, I had been too arrogant to do proper due diligence. Had I done so, the answer would have been obvious.

Every solution needs to meet the needs of the opportunity. It is just as important to understand the ins and outs of your solution as it is to understand the extended landscape and contours of the opportunity. Simply, I did not understand enough about the opportunity.

Avoid a business opportunity—or at least be very skeptical of one—that offers an answer to a question that no customer has asked. If you can find a lot of customers who are all wondering the same thing—why can't I do this?—you have a winner.

I found another job. I waited and learned. I broke things down until I could understand a project from one side to the other. It wasn't easy. I worked my ass off, frankly. But I did some real soul-searching and came up with the Four Rules. I decided that whatever happened from that point on—no matter what I did or who I did it with—I would commit to those four rules.

Simple. But it wasn't easy!

I was at the top of my class when it came to the street MBA. I wish I had been able to avoid bankruptcy and failure—no one likes to fail ... ever! It is never fun. But I realize it was necessary for me to learn what I needed to learn. I used that experience as a case study to model all my future decisions; in time and with a lot of effort and hard work, I was able to turn a thirty-five dollar investment into a technology company that ultimately employed over 2,000 employees and had sales of more than $220 million.

I owe all of it to the dismal failure of my first company.

We will talk later and at some length about core values and mission. But one thing we need to deal with right away: strategy. Yes, every business needs a strategy—the how of how things get done. But what you really need to remember is that you can never, and should never, confuse the mission of your business—the why of why you are in business—with the strategy.

When the horse dies, dismount.

If your strategy is not working, find a new one and fast. The "how" can change. The "why" can't.

A ten-point portrait of failure

I call Insta-Call my six month MBA because that is how long it took me to make every mistake possible (and some in retrospect almost impossible) to make in destroying my first business in six short months.

1) Did not understand the market (eat nothing bigger than your head).

2) Did not understand the technology evolution that would make my wooden kiosks irrelevant.

3) Had no understanding of the importance of positive cash flow. (Be prudent.)

4) Counted on my lawyers and accountants to give me confidence that I would be right and successful (banker's lunch).

5) Assumed starting a company was my goal, not building a company (never let your goals be your limitations).

6) Refused to admit I was wrong. Ego! I could have easily changed directions and started offering other services for traveling business people, but I didn't.

7) Failed to build up a trusted group of people who would support me (positive reputation).

8) Failed to build a company that would last forever.

9) Continued to party! Drank, smoked, caroused—even though I was captain of my own *Titanic*!

10) Took no accountability for my failure at first, which led to depression, bankruptcy and a minor heart attack (inner needs and core values).

Later in the book I will provide a ten-point counterpoint to this portrait.

It got better!

Chapter Three

Starting from Scratch and Getting It Right ... Finally

In the aftermath of Insta-Call, as I said, I spent the next twenty-eight months of my life examining every aspect of my Insta-Call failure and evaluating ways to ensure success the next time I started a company.

Fortunately I was hired as the general manager of a company called Reltek. Even though I had to go through the humiliation of bankruptcy and wage garnishment, I was safe in my new job. I had the chance to accept the truth— it was I who had failed, and not the system that had failed me—and to re-build myself both as a person and as an entrepreneur. And as I have come to believe deeply, the two are not distinct.

I worked very hard to develop more workable business models. I also came up with what I call my "acid tests for reality." Acid tests are what are used to distinguish real gold from fake. We'll review them in a later chapter, but think of them as the litmus test for what works for me. Not what works— *what works for me.* The difference is profound and you need to come to terms with the distinction. I say "no" to projects as often as I say "yes." Has that meant that I have walked away from money? Of course. But for me it has to be the right fit. I need a project or an idea to pass the test before I move on it. If a project passes three tests but fails a fourth?

Pass. Move on. There will always be new opportunities.

Another hugely important development in my mental renaissance was com-ing up with a reliable decision-making process that helped me build a com-pany that could last forever. I did it with Calian, and you can do it with your business too.

By responding to the pain and humiliation of rebuilding myself around my newly adopted values of success, I pressed those hard-learned lessons into service by starting Calian and proving them correct by being successful in making clear decisions and discerning the differences between business fact and fiction. The trauma of personal failure opened the door to change, and I walked through the door into another room full of hope. I had truly been altered by the beating I had taken. I was the same person yet somehow quite different in my actions, attitudes and business wisdom. The words that follow attempt to describe the tools I believe will help you build a company that can make you wealthy and secure.

The Space Cadet and the Street Fighter

Success comes in all shapes and sizes, colors, creeds and so on.

I mean this from the bottom of my heart: if I can succeed, anyone can. But what I hear most from people who are just starting out is, "Do I have what it takes?"

Okay, the short answer? Yes. You do if you believe you do. The longer answer is more complicated. Simple but not easy, right?

My experience is that we all have our strengths and weaknesses. We tend to focus more on our weaknesses and less on our strengths. Human nature, I guess. But I want you to think of yourself less as a collection of strengths and weaknesses and more as a toolbox. Let's say one person has a toolbox with everything but a hammer; another person has everything but a screwdriver. The point is, who we are and what we do well depends a lot on what needs to be done and when.

Enough of toolboxes.

I believe that anyone starting a business is going to need a combination of traits—and the irony is that the traits you need are diametrically opposed. This probably sounds like a diagnosis of schizophrenia. It isn't. A person starting a business needs to be a dreamer and risk taker and have a wonderful "devil may care" attitude. Meet the Space Cadet.

A startup is something outside a person's normal comfort zone. If you aren't capable of seeing past the risk, you won't succeed. At other times you must be the ruthlessly efficient street fighter or warrior who has the eyes of someone who would shoot first and is driven by the need to win. The Street Fighter will execute a plan or directive with chilling efficiency; he seldom starts a fight that is not already won before the gloves have come off.

Each trait on its own is not enough. You'll need both.

The pure Street Fighter—contrary to the name—doesn't really like to fight; he likes to win. The Street Fighter plays the odds; the better the odds, the more likely there will be a fight. Alternatively, the lower the odds of winning, the less likely a fight.

So, at the very beginning of your business, the Street Fighter might be more a liability than an asset. After all, he calculates, what is the point of fighting if you can't win.

On the other hand, the Space Cadet would leap to the challenge almost unaware of the consequences of failure. He would not worry about cash flow or overhead or mortgages, and he would never consider the possibility of failure.

Now, left on his own, the Space Cadet almost certainly will fail—and spectacularly. The Street Fighter, however, on his own will never get off his butt. He's the great idea that never gets off the ground.

I really believe we all have a bit of each inside us. Some have more of one and some have more of the other. The key is to know which is needed in what situation and how much.

So what does this mean for you?

Starting your own business—that critical first step—is a Space Cadet choice and you need to be 100 percent Space Cadet. Remember, too, that the biggest obstacle at the very beginning is not the market or even your competitor: it's you. So at the point of deciding that you want to start your own business, you need to be 100 percent Space Cadet.

It's David versus Goliath.

Hiring is another Space Cadet opportunity, as is any decision to extend a product line or expand your business.

Once the decision has been made, however, the Space Cadet must clear out and make room for the Street Fighter. Trust me, had Goliath survived that first fight and challenged David in a rematch, my money says Goliath would kick David's keester! Why? Goliath would have wised up to David's tricks. He would insist on rules that re-established the odds in his favour. No slings! No rocks!

Forget about the fairy tale of a level playing field. As a small business owner, you need to understand what your advantages are and use them. Once that "dream business" idea is a fact and a reality you need to switch into Street Fighter mode: you must be a tough son of a bitch evaluating and then eliminating every risk you see in front of you. So the 100 percent Street Fighter rules the roost—at least until the game suddenly changes and you need to make choices that require the Space Cadet to make those decisions take shape and crystallize. Once that decision is made and sold—either to you or your employees or your board—you need to mothball the Space Cadet and bring back the Street Fighter to defend those decisions to the death.

How can these two different traits co-exist in a single person? The truth is, it takes a lot of discipline to evoke these characteristics at any given time. In my case, I was a 100 percent Space Cadet when I started Insta-Call—and stayed a Space Cadet. The result? I had my head handed to me on a plate. It took me years to learn how to adjust the mix.

We all have our own personalities and our own biases. One person by nature is going to be more Space Cadet while another is going to be more Street Fighter. At the very beginning, this might not be such an issue. The smaller the company is, the more direct control you have over what goes on and the more your personality will prevail. But as your company expands and evolves it will develop layers; the risk is that the core mission can become diluted. You need to hire people for what they can do to continually reinforce the mission. Sometimes that will be the Street Fighter and other times it will be the Space Cadet.

It is important to understand people and what they do—and what needs to be done for the business to succeed and sustain that success over time. If you are in the stage of your business where you need a Street Fighter to knock sense into the market, don't hire someone who is more comfortable with the Space Cadet role. Likewise, don't expect the pure Street Fighter to dream big or "blue sky" effectively.

After Insta-Call I went to work for an old friend, Merv Sullivan. Merv owned Reltek Inc., a semiconductor-testing laboratory that he and a partner, Brian Crook, started in 1974. By 1980 their partnership had dissolved. Merv needed help and I needed a job. It was an ideal arrangement for both of us. Merv offered me 10 percent of the accounting profits for help rebuilding the company. I was back in the semiconductor business!

Testing semiconductor circuits is an extremely complicated task; happily for me and Merv, it was also mind-numbingly dull. The testing process was considered the most boring part of the electronics manufacturing process, and Reltek customers, for the most part, were happy—delighted—to pay someone else to do it.

This was a revelation to me. A real light-bulb moment—the Archimedean "ah ha!" It still is. I knew that our customers had the technological ability to test the circuits themselves, but they chose not to. Their interest was in funneling capital and intellectual resources into their core business.

I had discovered my first acid test!

Acid Test Number 1: provide a service that others either can't do or don't want to do; and even better if it is both.

Second option first: *do what others don't want to do.* This is a personal favorite of mine since it tends to be the most obvious.

Back in the seventies I had a great boss by the name of David Moore. He was a British semiconductor design superstar and probably one of the best designers in the world at the time.

Dave's septic system backed up one day and the quote he received for unclogging it was $150. Ever frugal and the consummate engineer, Dave figured he could design a better mousetrap. He figured he would get us grunts to do the laborious digging around the tank and that would save him a substantial chunk of change.

It was awful work. But we got the area dug out and all that seemed to be needed was the technician to show up and flip open the tank and clear it out. Dave was pretty pleased with himself.

In due course the technician showed up. He looked at us—mostly covered in dirt and muck—then at the hole and back at us. He flipped open the lid of the tank. The smell was like a punch in the face. He dropped it closed.

"A hundred fifty bucks. Cash."

Dave was taken aback. "But we've done a hundred dollars of work digging the tank clear."

The technician smiled. "Do you want the clog cleared? A hundred fifty bucks."

Dave paid up and the tank was cleared. I think that technician is still laughing.

Where there is muck, there's brass!

One of the biggest mistakes budding entrepreneurs make is assuming that opportunities are the consequence of innovation. That can certainly be true. Every new idea breeds opportunities. But what about established businesses? I call it my hammer paradox. Nothing looks quite as simple as a hammer. It just feels so *intuitive*. Perfect design. And it is. Or so we tend to believe. Have you thought about how you would redesign a hammer if you could?

You probably have a hundred or more interactions on a daily basis where you say to yourself, *I was not particularly pleased or happy with that experience.* Okay, there is your opportunity. What would you do to make that familiar exchange or experience more satisfying to the customer? Don't think of innovation as a product. Think of innovation as a state of mind. Look at the world around and use innovative thinking to *innovate*.

Sometimes the oldest trees in the garden yield the best fruit!

Most people starting out in business incorrectly assume that a shortage of funds is their biggest hurdle. That is true only if you want to start a business that has enormous start-up costs. So what would innovative thinking tell you? Avoid business opportunities with forbidding start-up costs and focus on services where time—hours worked—is more valuable than capital.

Calian would turn out to be a combination of option one and two. One, I found a niche opportunity that required a huge amount of expertise. Two, that same niche also happened to be something that no one wanted to do. *Where there's muck there's brass*? More like gold!

I always liked simple business opportunities that were not exciting or too sexy; the kind of venture that would not attract too much attention. Reltek was exactly that kind of business and it was run by one of the nicest and purest street fighters you would ever care to meet.

Merv Sullivan was a kind and humble man. He had a calm, pleasant way about him; every conversation started with a sincere question: "How are you doing?" He was truly interested. Merv was one of the smartest businessmen I ever knew but he was also the most humble. His ego could fit on the head of a pin. In the years I knew him, I never heard him utter a cross or mean word about anybody. Merv was a good man; he was the kind of boss you did not want to disappoint and I worked very hard for him during those twenty-eight months. He also had a very good business, and after my humiliating experience with Insta-Call I was in the mood to be around someone who was doing things right. I enjoyed everything about the company—even the customer complaints!

No matter how annoyed the customer was, I always thought: at least he has customers!

Merv and his wife, Jessica, ran a very frugal operation; every penny was counted, often twice, and once those pennies were counted they were his and he would keep his fist clenched around them as if his very life depended upon it. It was a wrestling match getting him to part with a dime. It didn't matter what it was for; even when he did agree he would toss pennies around like they were manhole covers. His mantra was simple: minimize expenditures and maximize benefit.

Simple!

Merv made sure that Reltek always got maximum value in any transaction. What so impressed me, though, besides his formidable intelligence, was that he wasn't greedy; he charged his customers fairly; he invested wisely; he never squandered his money. He fought for his company tooth and nail, of course; he was the classic street fighter. He was content not to take chances and was careful about money.

One time he asked if I wanted to go to the Cherry Hill testing conference in Philadelphia where all the major test equipment manufacturers showed their new testing products. I assumed we would fly the 450 miles but was stunned to find myself crammed into his six-year-old Honda Civic for a seven-hour ordeal that—typical of Merv—commenced at the end of a full eight-hour workday.

Merv was delighted that he had "saved a bundle" by driving.

Sadly, I simply could not face another seven-hour drive back and bought a one-way airline ticket. Hilariously, it turned out the costs of the two trips were about the same. Merv hadn't saved a bundle at all and I was spared the torture of being cooped up in a Honda Civic all day.

The whole next week Merv would not speak to me.

The point is not to make fun of Merv Sullivan. The incident taught me an important lesson about commitment—about what it means. It didn't matter to Merv in the end whether flying might have been cheaper. It was the principle that mattered.

It still does.

One more thing about Merv: as the pure Street Fighter, he was averse to risk. This was hard for me to understand at first; it ran against the image I had of the "risk taking entrepreneur" starting a business by defying the odds and becoming obscenely rich. Not Merv. He was allergic to risk. Years later I finally figured it out. The successful businessman is not a risk taker. He is a risk reducer. A new venture may look like a risk from the perspective of the outsider. But the risk-reducer is on the inside—or should be. That is a critical difference. Does Microsoft look like a risk from the perspective of 2013? No! How come? Because it wasn't a risk to Bill Gates back in 1979 when the company was founded. He knew what he had. When I started Calian I knew I had a great idea because I already had a market and I already had a service.

Here's what I mean.

One of the sideline businesses at Reltek was Quality Assurance (QA) consultancy. I had taken the company into this business without even asking Merv. It was the boring job of making sure all the paperwork and manual writing was done correctly to be in compliance with government contracting needs. It was slightly more profitable then the testing business, but it came with a number of risks, including some hard-to-define liabilities and the ultimate responsibility for the success of a project.

Merv had been unhappy with this business for a while; he considered the risks substantial. He was concerned that it put his testing business in jeopardy.

I thought otherwise. I believed the QA had a substantial upside in terms of profit and potential. True SF that he was, Merv did not think the potential warranted the risk; he wanted me to stop offering the service. To me, the business of providing QA consulting met my criteria of a good business: it was something others did not want to do themselves and that they would gladly pay for to have the headache removed. (Years later I would hear an MBA describe this phenomenon as "asymmetric market motivation." What better way to describe the difference between his and the street MBA approach!) It was quite clear to me that many small technology companies, including one that I had brought in called Dy-4 Systems, were about to win government contracts that would require this boring consulting help.

Merv did not want the risk of growing into a business where he saw the flaws and, like any true street fighter, chose the safer path. One of the other benefits of working at Reltek was that I got a keen idea of what kind of business was worth starting. Merv was right, of course, but I still had the drive to start a business, and this opportunity seemed better than most. A short time later Merv and I parted ways and I started Calian Technology to take advantage of the market opportunity that was in front of me.

A door closes for one but opens for another. Was there a risk for me? Not in the way you may think. Quality assurance services fell outside Merv's algorithm for what worked as a business model. I wanted to start my own business and it just so happened that QA services fell precisely within the frame of what constituted my business model.

Does that sound risky?

There is another lesson or two buried in that story. One is that not all businesses are designed to grow in the same way as others. You have to know what you want your business to be and—even more important—what you don't want it to be. How do you decide? Test it against your principles. A second lesson has to do with friendship and opportunity. Merv saved me. I owe him. He taught me a lot. But there came a time when I knew that who I wanted to be and what I wanted to do was no longer who or what Merv needed—or felt comfortable with. Don't force the round peg into the square hole.

Working for Reltek taught me how to identify a good business opportunity and I was on the prowl for an opportunity that would meet that simple criterion.

Chapter Four

Hire the Person ... Not the Resume

At first glance, 1982 seemed like the worst time to launch a new business. Prime interest rates were at a forbidding 10 percent, mortgages had ballooned to over 17 percent and the country was in a recession. The economic indicators were all bad and business managers all over Canada were "pulling in their horns" and defensively protecting their cash. It did not seem peculiar that the macroeconomic facts were at odds with the reality of a new clear and quantifiable customer list.

The world had changed, as well. The economy was moving from a resource and manufacturing to a resource and technology-based economy. The old rules did not seem to apply.

Not that it mattered. Calian was marching to the sound of a different economic drummer. Traditional industry was mired in a recession, but those of us in electronics and technology were experiencing an embarrassment of riches.

I had first met Kim Clohessy in the late seventies at the Greenway Glen squash club, a hang out for technology geeks, and we became fast friends. An Aussie, he enjoyed a good time, and over the years of playing squash and enjoying many a beer together, we got to know each other well. Kim had an enormously capable mind and a great sense of humor. As VP of engineering at Dy-4 Systems, he was the driving force behind what I thought was an exciting and dynamic company. The scope of his knowledge was very broad, and he could cut through the technical details faster than any young engineer I had ever met. DY-4 was at the forefront of the technology revolution; it had created traction in the new tech-oriented economy through a combination of specialized skills and aggressive management.

As I have said, I knew they were bogged down by QA compliance. I wanted Dy-4 to be the first customer in my new business.

We were both in our early thirties and living life to the fullest. Much of our social life revolved around a cottage we rented on magnificent Lake Calabogie. Many of our friends at the cottage were working in the technology sector. It wasn't hard convincing Kim to contract with my new company—whatever it would be called.

The cottage was owned by a sixty-year-retired government worker by the name of Norris (Curly) Pettis. Norris was a slow-talking, insightful, pipe-smoking man with the posture and overall demeanor of a Marine Corps drill sergeant. He walked with a slight limp due to "rusty pipes"—his euphemism for his clogged veins and arteries. Even so, he always had the walk of a man with purpose and a grace. As I would find out, he was also a very lucky man. He had flown thirty-nine bombing missions in WW II as a tail gunner in a Lancaster bomber. As a result he always seemed to be grateful for the little pleasures in life. Norris had a simple way of talking about problems that made the issues seem instantly clear.

In many ways he was my guiding light during the first five years of business. The lesson being that talent does not necessarily carry a briefcase or wear a nice suit.

I knew I had a great idea for a business. What I didn't have was a name. Since I had negotiated my first contract with Kim at Lake Calabogie I wanted a name that might memorialize the event. Calabogie, however, was not the most euphonious word. Calabogie Technology? That sounded awful. Boggy Technology? Even worse.

Norris suggested Calian Technology.

Perfect.

I had a name for my business and I had my first customer. I deposited thirty-five dollars in a new business bank account. And just like that I was back in business for myself. I just hoped I would make it past six months!

As part of my separation deal with Merv, he graciously allowed me to operate out of an office at Reltek for the first few months while I got the company up and running. Business was brisk. I had been right about my hunch that companies would be glad to pay me to take on tasks they considered onerous or even boring—like writing QA manuals and dealing with compliance and regulation requirements.

Before long, business had grown so much that I was able to rent a larger office in town. The building was owned by a local businessman named Don Armstrong. Every month when I hand-delivered my rent cheque I would talk to Don about business and very quickly I realized he had exceptional judgment.

An important lesson I learned is never to underestimate the value of a trusted mentor. Nothing is more obvious than that as human beings we all make mistakes. The best and most valuable mentors are the ones who are confident enough in their success—at home enough in their own skin—that they can share their war stories with you. But it's not just advice; it's being open enough and honest enough to take advice. I asked Don's advice on many issues—from people problems to contracts—and he never varied from a simple value system that was similar to my four rules.

By 1985 annual sales reached $187,000 and projects were headed for $787,000! Not bad for work that everyone else thought was boring!

As Calian grew, Don and a group of investors became interested in making an investment. In October 1985, I had the opportunity to make a presentation in Ottawa to all the members of the investment clubs at the esteemed old Laurentian Club. Accompanying me to the meeting were two early partners, Jack Wilson and Ed Lambert, who both had joined Calian in the first year. Unfortunately, as CEO I had to do all the talking.

It was my first financial presentation and I was so nervous that I had to sit down to complete the presentation. A major component of the company's future growth would be a product called the AQOP-1000, which used computer discs to store military standards and specifications. Another was a new quality management system called Bloodhound. As the name implied, it tracked down subcontractors who were not meeting or had failed to meet contractual obligations. I was telling the group how Calian was going to automate what had been a paper-intensive record-keeping process of quality assurance on a new contract for a military ship being built at the Saint John Ship yards in New Brunswick. The investors were, for the most part, local Ottawa business people who, like Don, sensed something unusual and exciting was happening in the economy and wanted to make sure they had a piece of the action.

The next day Don told me that they had agreed to invest $100,000 in Calian. Believe it or not, a huge vote of confidence for Calian as a safe bet for investment was that I had launched another business before Calian and failed.

I called Norris Pettis with the good news. By that time Norris was spending one day a week in Ottawa helping me with the books and numerous other administrative chores.

The investment came just in time. Ed Lambert had just won another federal government contract and—as fantastic as that was—a new contract was going to stretch our cash reserves. At the rate we were going we'd be out of cash by Christmas. The new $100,000 investment would stabilize our situation until the earnings from the new contract started to turn into real cash. Ed was doing an exceptional job. He had a wizard's touch when it came to writing and winning long-term lower-margin contracts that created a much more predictable business flow than the smaller contracts revolving around quality assurance projects. (If any single individual can be singled out for contributions made during those early years, it was Ed Lambert.)

Ed Lambert was a big man who, in his youth, could bench-press 300 pounds; in another day he had been a military police officer tasked with guarding nuclear weapons in Germany. Before he became an employee of Calian, I invited him out to lunch one day to talk about government contracting. He was working for Ian Martin, a competitor at the time. The lunch was cordial and brief. The consummate professional, he had no interest talking "out of school." I had given him my best Calian pitch but he wouldn't bite. I was disappointed, of course, but I deeply respected his integrity and business savvy.

It turned out we had a lot in common. He, too, had tried and failed at business and was more than happy to talk about the mistakes he made in life and work. We had a very good meeting; I liked Ed and I was sorry I could not tempt him away to work for me. I resigned myself to the not entirely unworthy thought that in Ed Lambert I had a more than capable adversary with whom to contend!

Walking out of the restaurant after lunch, we shook hands. I laughed about something he said and were about to go our separate ways when we both saw his boss from Toronto walking into the very same restaurant. The next day I went to a government bidder's conference for a contract—a contract at the time held by Ed's company—and I sat at the table directly across from Ed's boss, who glared at me during the entire meeting.

Ed was fired that afternoon.

Two weeks later Ed was working for Calian as Government Operations Director (GOD as we joked). Although we were both pigheaded and fought over almost every issue, it was a truly good working relationship. Ed had one failed business in his past and had also grown up in a tough family situation. He was honest and could talk about his mistakes.

Hiring can be the most difficult and perplexing aspect of any small business. But it doesn't have to be. First, don't be afraid to look for talent outside the normal channels. Of course you don't want someone in accounts who can't add or subtract. But there are very few skills that cannot be learned. But a resume or CV can be a very poor indicator of what a person can do. People who have failed—people who have fallen on their ass—often are the people who have something to prove. That led me to the discovery of my second acid test.

Acid Test Number 2: never hire someone who will not admit a mistake

Trust is difficult—in life but especially in business.

Ask yourself—and be honest—in your own life how many people do you trust? I mean really trust?

One of the most reliable ways I have found of creating trust is by hiring people who will admit to having made mistakes. First, it's an admission you might think makes you look bad. And it does—if you are the kind of person who consistently makes mistakes and especially the same kind of mistakes. But what I look for is the person who is honest about the mistakes he or she has made because the person has learned from the failure. Failure is inevitable; what is not inevitable is the person who—having tumbled from the ladder—climbs back up. That person has shown me something valuable— something you will never find on a resume.

I need to know that I am surrounding myself with people who believe that mistakes—even failure—can lead to greater success in the future as long as the person is able to deal with the truth. Success has its obvious rewards: fancy cars, a nice house, a boat, whatever. Those are all external and easily visible. Failure is less obvious and tends to be almost exclusively internal. For me failure became the fuel that powered my engine to succeed. As I have said before, people who have failed and refuse to quit generally have something to prove. Those are the people with the proverbial "fire in the belly."

A question I often asked during a job interview for a position at Calian was, "What is the biggest mistake you have ever made in your life?"

The reaction to this question was always a revelation and often provided a deep insight into the workings of someone's mind and sometimes even indirectly his or her soul.

Interestingly, a much-higher-than-average percentage of candidates tended to smile or laugh uncomfortably and hem and haw or wrinkle their forehead in thought.

"Hmmm. Let me think about that ..."

Were I to be asked that same question I wouldn't hesitate. I would narrate my Insta-Call disaster chapter and verse. And what would that tell the guy

31

across the desk? Not that I love talking. No, it would reveal to the person that I had failed and had spent a lot of time figuring out why, and that I was determined never to make that mistake again! It would reveal that the reason I want to work for you is that I need to prove to you and to me and to everyone else that I have what it takes.

So, between candidate A who wants the job because of the salary and the benefits or candidate B who wants to prove he has the right stuff, who do you think won't need to be motivated?

That simple question was an acid test I used very successfully to discern many things about a prospective employee. You could find out if they were honest and humble enough to talk freely about their failures. Failure could be a spectacular chance to learn and grow and I needed people around me who were not afraid to admit they could fall short. Making an error of judgment was one thing—blaming it on someone else another. I was never embarrassed to follow this line of questioning, often with surprising results.

After all, by the time I started to ask that question of myself, I had a list of failures as long as my arm and I was not afraid of talking and in some cases even bragging about my misadventures. I felt that the mistakes I had made along the way had given me permission to use every weapon in my arsenal not to make another mistake in the hiring process. I could learn a great deal about someone with that simple single question: "Tell me about your biggest mistake."

This question is harmless enough if answered directly and quickly—honestly and with complete humility. As I said, often I would see eyes suddenly darting for the exit, or the candidate would be struck by a spontaneous case of complete memory loss. Some candidates even broke out into floppy sweats. It's understandable: for the most part we live in a meritocracy (I said for the most part!) where achievement is rewarded and failure shunned. We tend to spin things towards what we think we have done right and away from what we have done wrong. If they only knew, however, why the question was actually asked! I was not only interested in their achievements, but in their level of self-awareness. Simply having admitted to being a mere mortal would have been the end of it; I would have moved away from that line of questioning, but some chose to drag it out and I always—I hate to admit it—quite enjoyed the process (some would probably call it an interrogation!).

The really unfortunate candidate would try and pretend that he or she had never really made a mistake. That would always bring to life my dark and cruel side. I would toy with my prey for a while —dragging it out—before finally and mercifully ending the interview. I had series of torturous questions that could eventually tighten the noose around even the most defensive personality.

If it was an engineer, the line of questioning might focus on the candidate's amazing ability to design every circuit right "first time!" If it was a salesperson I could explore the candidate's 100 percent customer-retention rate and marvel at how fantastic that was for him and his last company. Eventually, each would come to understand that what I was after was the simple truth—the business truth and not the business fiction. Under the relentless pressure the candidate would bring forth a supposed mistake or failure.

Just once I would have loved an answer to "what was your biggest mistake?" to be something like "not having honestly answered that same question at my last interview"!

An extremely valuable insight for any business owner is having some insight into what another person considers a big mistake. Was it a mistake that took them back to their university days and revolved around taking the wrong major? Was the slip that really stuck in their mind twenty years later that they should have taken economics 201 instead of accounting? Those who remained in that time warp could still be very valuable employees, but that certainly was not high on my priority list of mistakes.

A career choice blunder or personal relations blunder was closer to the mark. These kinds of situations would give some insight into the relationship they saw between themselves, the company and their fellow employees. This direction was always useful since it gave a much clearer idea about where they did not want to go again and whether that direction fit with Calian's needs. Yes, a career gaffe was good enough not to stop the interview but it still wasn't the perfect type of mistake for me to hear. The best mistake to discuss with me was a pure business error. Preferably, it was a blunder that had ended in disaster.

A business mistake was music to my ears. A candidate who admits to having taken his last company into a market that wasn't real and in the process had learned the hard way the difference between a good and a bad business idea.

Bingo!

A contrite look might flash across his face at some point in the discussion and that was a very good sign. The recollection of the mistake or failure still stung—it still had the power to motivate. If the words and the music were in harmony, I would become the champion of the hiring process. I suspect my colleagues often must have thought I was nuts.

This candidate just admitted to having committed a gigantic blunder that cost his company a fortune. What are you so happy about?

Yes, making a big business mistake was something to be savoured: the lessons learned from every mistake would help an individual succeed. And remember, the most important information about the mistake is not that it was made; it's that it was admitted and this person is highly motivated never to do it again!

Humble people who had failed and had been upfront about it became the building blocks of Calian; without them our company could never have grown. Remember what St. Augustine said: *hate the sin but not the sinner*. In business the forgiveness of an honest mistake is the first step to becoming an ethical businessperson. With this knowledge came a peace.

Ed Lambert was one of those people. He was a rainy day man who always came through for Calian. Although he left Calian in the early nineties, he was one of the early partners that made a long and lasting impression on the future of Calian.

While we're on the topic: bankers

Never buy your banker lunch.

Huh?

I remember one time—actually, quite a few times—sitting at expensive restaurants with my banker or lawyer or accountant or whomever. The cheque would arrive and I would always make the grab. Then one day I thought, *O'Brien, what the heck are you doing? Who is powering this train? Me? or my banker?*

Okay, when starting up your own business your inclination will be to turn to as much advice and expertise as you can. Knowledge is a beautiful thing— don't get me wrong. After all, I am hoping this book will give you some good advice! But never forget that you are your best resource. We have lost touch with our instincts. Elsewhere I call this common sense.

As your business grows, there will be new and more complex issues and problems to deal with. You will need to adapt—but not change! You will find yourself hiring accountants and managers, consulting with bankers and investors or experts from here, there and everywhere. They will all have tons of advice. What a relief!

Wrong!

Bankers and other professionals have their place in business. But let me make it very clear: they can take more money out the back door with teaspoons than you will ever be able to bring in the front door with a shovel.

A ten-point portrait of success

In an earlier chapter I listed my ten-point portrait of failure. With a lot of hard work I managed to turn things around. What made the difference—besides the hard work—was my commitment to the four values.

Here's the difference:

1) I started Calian doing something that my customers did not want to do for themselves. The bonus was that I knew I had the expertise to do what needed to be done.

2) I worked hard to build a company that was on a solid and sustainable growth curve.
   Talk about long term!

3) I started Calian with a $35 deposit into my Calian bank account. That was the last money I ever invested. I didn't eat anything bigger than my head!

4) I concentrated on positive cash flow and never used an accountant, lawyer or anyone else during the first few years except for taxes etc. I became very prudent with my dollars.

5) I started Calian with the goal of building a company that would go public in ten years.

6) I took personal responsibility for every action and mistake the company took or made and worked tirelessly to correct every mistake and right every wrong.

7) Honesty was my only choice; good or bad, I always searched for the truth and I always tried to do the just and honorable thing in every situation. That built and sustained my reputation. It created trust and allowed me to be a successful leader.

8) I made it my goal to build a company that would last forever and I surrounded myself with like-minded people who shared and supported the mission.

9) I stopped drinking for the first two years of building Calian and lived like a monk and worked eighty to ninety hours a week.

10) I ruthlessly autopsied my failures and made sure I took a positive lesson from each and every one. Just as important, I committed myself to those new positive values.

Chapter Five

To Do or Not to Do? Making Wise Choices

Whether you are a CEO with thirty years' under your belt or small business owner just starting out, you will be bombarded by choices. And the reality is, there is no escape. There is never any place to hide.

Not if you want to stay in business.

You've probably heard it said that business is a minefield—one false step and your business is blown sky high. Here's what I say: they're right!

As a business owner, you need to make thousands of choices and as your company grows the kinds of choices will change and challenge your decision-making process. But what the Prophets of Doom do not tell you is this: learn how to make good choices from the very beginning and you can ride out whatever comes down the pike. My experience has been that too few people have enough confidence to stick with a decision-making process in the first place. What should be a "yes" or a "no" increasingly becomes a "maybe" as you find yourself doubting your own intuition and experience and surrendering to fashionable or trendy shortcuts. Back to the short-term as opposed to the long-term, right?

The wrong "yes" or "no"—assuming the decision has passed the acid tests outlined here—will be either a victory or a setback. But remember: no victory is permanent and neither is a setback. Enjoy your victory, but don't dwell on it. Likewise, break down the mistake and figure out where you went wrong with the acid tests. And move on.

A "maybe" in business is like a bad opera: it isn't really singing and it isn't really drama but some weird in-between thing that no one in the audience understands or is happy with. Don't be afraid to make mistakes. Make sure you make a mistake for the right reason. If a decision needs to be postponed, don't just walk away from the table. You as the business leader need to make clear to everyone concerned why the decision is being delayed and what needs to be known in order for that decision to be made. And put that decision back on the calendar.

To me the beauty of the four values is that—bottom line—they are really four perspectives on the same value: do what is right. Do unto others, right? Big decision, small decision, whatever, it should always be the same. Ask yourself, in the long run who is ultimately responsible for every decision that I will make for my business? Right. You. So learn how to listen to that voice inside your head that will keep you and your business focused on the horizon. Do what is right.

Two things I want you to remember at all times. First, never assume you know more than you do. Arrogance in business is poison. Frankly, it isn't a particularly pleasant trait to come upon in life either. (At the end of the day, wouldn't you agree that it is the humble man who seems most happy and contented with himself? Arrogance requires the forced complicity of others. It wastes resources and fogs up the business culture you should be working every day to nurture and sustain.) Two, and this is really the flip side of the first thought: never pretend you don't know what you need to know. If there is one thing we have in surplus, it's information. Use it. Think of every decision as a kind of beaker into which a required amount of liquid is contained. No more and no less.

I'm not sure is not an option. *Maybe* is not an option.

The world seems more complex every day. How are we supposed to navigate our way? It all seems way too complex for any one person to understand, right? Well, that's what we are told anyway. So we surrender our authority—and by authority I mean what used to be called "common sense" or "instinct"—to this strange hybrid called the "expert" or the "consultant" or "meetings" where topics are discussed to death and nothing is accomplished.

A third ruled of decision-making: if you need a consultant you don't know enough about your business to be in business. The follow-up to that is: know your customer. A consultant or an expert will charge you a fortune to tell you what you should already know. A customer will tell you for free what you need to know.

This is especially true for the start-up entrepreneur. Yes, of course you need wise counsel. You need to do your due diligence. Exactly what I so spectacularly failed to do my first time out. Think of it like this: at some point every day in our lives we are a customer. In fact, we spend most of our waking life as a customer. What has your experience as a customer been? Are you satisfied? If not, how come? What would you do differently if you had the chance? These simple questions are the foundation upon which you should be building your decision-making process. The more you ask and explore, you more you will connect with what is right.

At the very beginning it is much easier to make decisions in some ways. It's only you, right? Some decisions work and some don't. Hopefully you have more right decisions than wrong decisions and your business grows. But then something funny happens: you see growth and expansion—even success—as inevitable. And why not? It's easy to get complacent. The problem is, don't let that complacency cloud the decision-making process.

For instance, ask your employees why your product is superior to your competitor's. What would they say? Ask them to tell you how the service they provide is superior to what your competitor is supplying?

If you are making the right decisions about your business and its culture—its mission—they will have answers at the ready. If not, you are in serious trouble. Because that ladder that you climbed up on your way to success? A bunch of hungry people are right behind you on that ladder.

Always listen. It sounds so simple, right? Trust me, it's the hardest thing in the world. Listen to everyone around you. Listen to your customers. Learn to listen to that valuable voice inside your head that is telling you whether or not you are doing the right thing. And I hate to be sexist, but the fact is that men tend to be lousy listeners. Men like to think they are problem solvers. It's a contest. Men don't want to read maps; they think they can intuit the goal on their own. Only wimps use maps, right?

So what happens? Right, they end up lost. Ego, arrogance ... whatever. People who don't listen couldn't find their way around in a glass of water. Now, women may make the same error but in the opposite direction. They put a high value on group discussion and consultation. Adequate preparation. Contingency plans. Great qualities. The most important element in a business strategy besides good decision-making is execution. No sense making good decisions if you don't have the people on board who know how to implement those decisions and insinuate them into your business culture.

But just like in the Street Fighter and the Space Cadet examples, the key is finding the right mix. The seat-of-the pants driver who never uses a map will not generally arrive at the predetermined goal. On the other hand, occasionally they end up somewhere wonderfully unexpected. Too much discussion about a decision can be as toxic as too little. Someone willing to read a map might have known that the almost invisible black line on the map is really a deep canyon before driving over the edge. With too much discussion, the necessary bias every business owner must have to make a timely decision is lost in committee. Mappers may be inclined to follow a route so literally that they miss the opportunity for improvisation. The point of this is not to get mixed up in gender debate. I have come upon as many men who are "map readers" as women who are "seat of the pants" drivers.

As the business owner you need to be the decision maker. The decisions you make need to be respected, they need to implemented, they need to be understood, and they need to be consistent.

Not consistently wrong. Consistent. People who work for you need to know that their voices will be heard and considered. But once that has happened, you as the decision maker need to decide. No more discussion. Decision time. Don't put it off. Don't ever allow yourself to be seen trying to escape the responsibility of deciding. Never allow yourself to be seen improvising a decision. Be consistent.

Would you trust a contractor who suddenly decided he wanted to adjust the height of one wall on a blueprint? Heck no! And remember, whether you have a small business or a large business, it does not matter if everyone agrees with your decision. What they do need to agree on, however, is that it is consistent. Inconsistent decision-making invites doubt. Doubt is destabilizing. It distracts from the mission.

A wrong decision can be corrected—as long as the correction itself seems consistent.

It is even more important that your company build on good choices. Not week-to-week but over many years. You will find that consistently making good decisions—otherwise known as making consistent decisions—over the years will build both a positive reputation and a network of like-minded colleagues who will be with you through the process of building a company that will last forever.

I said that after the Insta-Call debacle I went through a long and deep process to figure out what had gone wrong with my decision-making strategy. It turned out to be so simple! A successful business is not based on a single idea or a single decision but hundreds if not thousands of choices that needed to be made quickly and efficiently. And where had I gone wrong? For one thing, I didn't really have a strategy. What I had was an idea on steroids. I was so juiced on my own brilliance that it blinded me to even the simplest due diligence. What did my potential customers think of my brilliant idea? Not much!

This was an important insight because I realized I needed a framework to test my solutions and—more important—to immunize them against the toxic effects of ego. At Insta-Call I would come up with many solutions to any given problem, but I did not have a value framework to compare the various solutions. I never tested them against a framework of values that would enhance the probability of success.

Acid Test Number 3: test every major choice you make against the four values

We first encountered the four values in Chapter One and I don't want to plough old fields. But this acid test is so important that it really should be number one. If you memorize the four values and follow the strategy faithfully, I guarantee you success. Whenever you have a number of options to solve a specific business problem, test the solutions with these questions.

- Is it an honest solution? Do you have the truth?
- Is it a long-term solution?
- Does it add value to your company, your customers and your employees?
- Is it prudent? Are you wasting energy or money?

You will get good at testing the solutions you are choosing and it will become second nature. Remember that success is not one decision but thousands made over years of simple yet hard work

Chapter Six

You Can't Do It Alone: the Value of People

By 1990, Calian had pulled away from the pack. We had really come into our own.

A decade earlier, US President Ronald Reagan had initiated a more than trillion-dollar increase in defence spending and Calian was poised perfectly to cash in on the boom. During those early years, Calian was active in Canadian programs such as Low Level Air Defence (LLAD) and the Canadian Patrol Frigate Program (CPF) as well as numerous other small programs that were part of the overall race to bankrupt the Soviets.

The increase of defence spending was North America's single major political event of the eighties, followed only by the growth in computer technology.

The new technologies were speeding up the way the world communicated, and by the end of the decade just about everyone had a PC on their desktop and e-mails were beginning to replace memos as a means for executives to vector information. The eighties had been an interesting—and for me and my colleagues at Calian—an incredibly lucrative decade.

By 1990, Ottawa had 27,534 technology workers at 300 firms creating wealth and changing Ottawa and Canada. Calian employed about 80 people and had even opened a small office in Washington D. C. where we did support work for Canada, Australia and Spain in the defence sector. We had become a real company! More important, my second son, Matthew Donald, arrived in the summer of 1990.

Life was good. And as I would soon learn, it was about to get even better. But maybe not for the reason you think. Let me explain.

But first ... a bit of background

Two years before, a larger and more established rival in our field had offered to buy me out.

To be honest, their offer was incredibly generous. I was stunned. My first thought was, *yes*! I had survived a disastrous bankruptcy and hospitalization and depression only to have picked myself up and built my own company from the ground up. And here were the Big Boys of my industry offering me a pot of money to sell.

When a company like Science Applications International Corp (SAIC) makes a just offer, it is very hard to ignore them. SAIC was an American technology company with sales in the US approaching $700 million in 1987. SAIC was founded in 1969 to serve the military and other government agencies with advanced technology services.

SAIC wanted into the Canadian defence and security market and hired the retired, golf-playing three-star general Ernie Crebber to help get SAIC established. Ernie was well respected by the Canadian defence establishment and was an excellent choice as president of SAIC Canada. He introduced the concept of acquiring Calian in the summer of 1987, and after a few chats we had a non-binding letter of agreement, which was signed that fall. I soon found myself in detailed negotiations with an American by the name of Joseph E. Murray Jr. , an ex-navy officer who in fact ran the operations side of SAIC Canada. Joe was a hard-driving manager who wanted to rise in the ranks of SAIC, and Calian was definitely a stepping-stone to his advancement. As we got closer to a binding agreement, I realized that I had absolutely no experience in buying or selling a company and that was going to be a problem.

I was negotiating with a company that had grown by acquisition—and they were very good at the process. I was at a serious disadvantage. I was a true virgin. There is an old saying I remembered which was appropriate to this situation: "When a man with experience and no money negotiates with a man with money and no experience, an exchange occurs: the man with the money ends up with the experience and the man with the experience ends up with the money!"

If I was to survive the process of acquisition, I needed experience and I needed it quickly. Fortunately I had experienced people startlingly close at hand.

One of the most important advisors I had was my then father-in-law, Don Green. Don had sold a few of his own companies and he was a deft hand at how business really works. He was also someone I deeply respected—not just for his success but for his value system. He asked me a question that seemed innocent enough at the time but would haunt me later. "How was I going to like working for a big company?"

No problem, I assured him.

I remember he smiled and nodded.

I met with my closest colleagues to discuss the impending deal. Reviews were mixed. Two—Don Armstrong and Norris Pettis—believed it was premature to sell Calian. They thought the company had not reached its potential. However, they both insisted that they would not stand in the way if that is what I wanted to do. Don asked me to have lunch with a friend of his, David Fleck, who was a skilled and experienced negotiator.

It was an inspired introduction. David turned out to be a wizard of the negotiation process. He even managed to squeeze another $300,000 of value for the employees and shareholders. It was a heady and instructive tutorial. The process itself can be mind-numbingly complex but bizarrely seductive. Over time I actually became quite enchanted by the acquisition process. In fact, I earned my second six-month MBA course over that period.

Months later the negotiations wrapped up and we made plans for signatures to finalize the deal. I was very proud of myself. I was elated!

Then something very odd happened.

I began to have serious doubts.

"Mr. O'Brien? It's your conscience calling. Do you want to take it?"

I can still feel the chill of that icy morning in March as I looked around my office.

I was literally a simple signature away from the biggest and most lucrative deal of my life. Two accountants from the Price Waterhouse accounting firm and a battery of lawyers were huddled in the boardroom reviewing the acquisition agreement. And all I could think of was, what the heck am I doing?

Calian and I had grown up together in these offices. We had built a wonderful business. I had many trusted and valued colleagues and employees. A family. Instead of feeling happy about the acquisition, I felt suddenly lost and at loose ends.

The night before, I had taken a late night walk with Ballie, my faithful golden retriever. Actually, several walks. Poor Ballie. She must have wondered what my problem was.

"Would you figure out what you want to do already?" I imagine she whimpered. "It's cold out here!"

I did know what I wanted to do. Had to do. Maybe I had known it all along. I screwed up my courage and walked to the boardroom.

"Get out," I announced. "It's over. No deal. Calian is not for sale."

I remember there was some awkward and nervous laughter, like I had made a bad joke. The lawyer and accountants just stared at me with owlish, disbelieving eyes. "I am not selling Calian to SAIC! Do not waste your money checking my books and legal papers. Just get out!"

I looked at each person around the table. I must have had my most menacing Street Fighter face on because the room went suddenly deadly quiet.

Their heads swiveled from one to another. I think this maniac is serious! the look on their faces betrayed.

Damned right, I was serious.

They started to frantically gather up papers and binders and were hustled out the door.

I took a deep breath. I had just scotched a huge deal. The biggest deal of my life. I had turned my back on millions of dollars. I felt wonderful. Better than I had ever felt in my life.

Ed Lambert, aka GOD, our hulking government operations director, walked up to me.

"Thank you," he said. That's it. We left the boardroom and went back to work—back to our mission of making Calian the best company it could be.

Okay, sweet story. But what the heck happened? What made me change my mind? Fair enough.

As I said, the night before I found myself unable to think about anything but the long and unfolding saga of Calian over the last five years. It felt like a dream. Life had changed so much since a thirty-two-year-old bankrupt technologist decided to try business "one more time" and founded a consulting company on an investment of his last thirty-five dollars. It was madness! Building Calian from scratch had consumed tens of thousands of hours. And not only my own hours: I had many people—many wonderfully talented and dedicated people—who shared my enthusiasm and passion and who worked with me hour for hour, day in and day out. We all had a stake in the dream … the dream of building a company that would last forever.

Remember I began this story by saying life was about to get better for me but maybe not for the reason you might think?

This is so trite that it is almost embarrassing to admit: but I realized something standing alone outside on that cold March night at four in the morning with my dog and my thoughts. It really isn't about the money. It's about the people.

It always has been and it always will be.

So often and in so many ways that are largely lost to time, it would be the people around me who would prove most crucial to my success. I would be in the process of mulling over some ticklish or perplexing problem and someone like General Bill Casley would come up to me and say, "Keep an even keel in the water boy" and cleverly guide me to another solution. Bill had joined Calian in 1986 as chair of the Calian board and I never heard a negative word from him. He has been one of the steadiest and wisest hands I have ever known. Calian had grown from a one-person start-up to being a take-over opportunity because of our people and our culture.

Calian had many parents—every person who worked with me from the very beginning shared a commitment to the same core values: honesty, long-term thinking, adding value and prudence.

Look, Calian was my company. But it became a lot of people's company. I am not evangelizing on the idea that all companies have to succeed this way. This is the way I used a system to build a company that will last. You don't have to do it this way.

Could things have worked out had I sold Calian and it had become part of a larger company? Sure. But when the internal needle on your compass—that inner decision-maker we all have—tells you one thing and you are doing another … it's decision time. My needle was pointing to what my father-in-law was getting at when he asked me if I would be happy working for someone else. He didn't ask me if I would be richer. Would I be happy?

To be honest, in the end the decision was not hard to make. It was easy. I realized that by obeying my conscience—by following my four values—I had not closed the door to a windfall. I had opened a new door to something much better and a lot more worthwhile.

It's up to you. It's your business. It's you who has to decide.

Honesty is your best insurance policy

Shortly after the last minute cancellation of the SAIC acquisition, I received a call from a colleague's wife. Calian had been providing Millar Communications Systems with QA consulting services for a number of years. Allan Millar had been diagnosed with dementia related to Alzheimer's. I had known Allan for years. But when his wife said Allan was sick, things began to make sense. Allan had been behaving oddly. I would often get calls from him in which he would go on talking about things I had little knowledge of or that made little or no sense.

It turned out that MCS was having some problems. The Miller family would have to sell MCS. I offered whatever help I could.

For starters, I put them in touch with David Fleck. He shopped the company around but with little success. None of the large defence and communications companies wanted to buy a small $3-million contract research company whose president and chief rainmaker was sick and in a legal battle over the company's major technology contracts. It was a tough sell.

One evening David phoned me with a proposition. He wanted me to buy Miller Communication and in a novel way that would allow the Miller family to maximize the return on the sale. It was no secret that Allan's medical bills would eat up a lot of the profits from a sale and we wanted to make sure the family was secure. We quickly agreed to terms. To be honest, the issue of price hardly entered the conversation. It came down to what would benefit the family most.

A few months later, the paperwork was signed. The Miller family was delighted that Allan's "baby" would stay in the family, so to speak. And I felt really good about their long-term peace of mind. I owned MCS. It was a considerable reversal of direction for me and for Calian. I had gone from a seller of Calian to a buyer of MCS in three months. Calian was about to take a definite turn that would lead to the company offering systems engineering and advanced satellite communications and a future that I could never have dreamed possible.

Allan passed away a few years later.

It turned out that Allan had a $500,000 life insurance policy that would pay out to MCS directly and not to the family. As Calian owned MCS, that meant the money would come to us. At the time, Calian was short of cash. The Calian board of directors insisted that Calian had every right to the money. To be fair, the board was following sound business practice.

Okay, but was its insisting on a legal right to an unexpected windfall a sound short-term and a sound long-term decision?

First, ethically I believed that it had been Allan's intention that the policy was to benefit his wife and family by protecting his most obvious asset: MCS. In short, my inner voice—my core value system—was telling me that collecting on the insurance money was not the ethical thing for the company to do. Second, and this may seem a bit unfeeling under the circumstances—but as CEO I had to decide what the real value of the windfall would be to Calian.

Yes, it would relieve us of what I thought was an unenviable but temporary cash shortage. The key, of course, was the temporary. How would Calian benefit in the long-run. Would its reputation be enhanced or damaged?

As I said, Allan was a much admired and respected figure. It was known that Calian had come to his rescue at a time of need. The purchase of MCS also put Calian on the map with players in the technology industry in Canada. MCS was small, but it had worked on just about every major research project and advanced communications system in Canada.

The respect the business community had for Allan became an opportunity for me to earn that same respect. I worked long and hard to make sure it was known to MCS's customers that they were appreciated and valued. The acquisition of Miller—a small but trusted company—also enlarged my staff by about twenty-five highly competent and experienced engineers and technologists.

I needed approval from the board to void the insurance payout to Calian. To be honest, there was more of a debate than I would have preferred. In the end, however, I prevailed. A big reason why, I believe, is that I focused on the long-term advantages: enhanced reputation, improved market presence, increased talent pool, expanded contacts, and so on. As I explained to the board, isn't all that worth $500,000? Turn down the money now and we turn on the money faucets down the road. That sounds crude. I don't mean it to be. Allan was a dear friend.

But as a business owner, you will find that you cannot afford to let your feelings get the upper hand. Business—like nature—is not sentimental. You have to make decisions that are best for the company. But what I am promising you is this: follow the four values and you will find that the right thing to do is the same thing as the right thing to do for the company.

Chapter Seven

Turning Points, or, How Could I Have Been So Stupid?

All businesses have them—doesn't matter how big or how small. The turning point. And I say "the" specifically to distinguish the singular determining turning point from a turning point, otherwise known as the millions of bends and curves that are the routine of business life. There is a turning point in any company's history that defines the success or failure of a legacy. There is always that one moment, that one event, which is to be savored or scorned when reflected upon. It is the "how could I have been that lucky?" or "how could I have been so stupid?" moment. In my case, it was a meeting in July 1990 with two executives from a much larger company— SED Systems of Saskatoon—which I was negotiating to acquire.

That meeting changed the future of Calian. I was at the table and it suddenly hit me like a ton of bricks: these two executives held the key.

Ray Basler was the junior of the two. He had already displayed to me an incredible capacity for mastering complex financial detail while grasping the substantial business issues and problems of an acquisition. He could shift and refocus his mind from big picture to detail in an instant and could summarize pages and pages of financial data into a few lines with frightening efficiency. His skills were awesome and I realized that in his wheelhouse I was simply no match. His quick wit and sense of humour, however, always put me at ease.

The other executive, Dugald Buchanan, was a gunfighter. He was direct and never wasted or minced words. He had been late to the meeting because his wife, Cindy, was having their second child. We had that in common as my own second son had been born the month before. Dugald had both the experience and instincts to negotiate a tough deal with me. Clearly his priority was maximizing the benefit for him and his management team. I took that as a given, but I still had the confident feeling that he could be trusted. I knew in my heart that if an agreement was reached to benefit all of us, I would have his 100 percent support. Dugald was the kind of guy who could take your back in a bar fight.

"Just so we understand it clearly," he said, sounding like a man who had been lied to before. "If we drop our plans for a management buy-out (MBO), our team of nine managers will own 10 percent of Calian and get 20 percent of the cash flow profits from SED?"

"Yes, that would be right," I answered. "And I will need your help and all your support." I went on to describe my thoughts about how the transaction might be able to work.

First, I needed them to drop their own plans and join Calian's attempt at bidding on SED. Calian could bring an Ottawa and federal government presence to SED; we could also raise cash if needed. These factors would allow them to reduce their risks by joining Calian. Then, of course, we would have to negotiate with three parties: Fleet, the current owner; the government of Saskatchewan, which held all the debt and therefore all the cards; and the federal government. It was no wonder that so many other companies had looked at SED and decided to walk away. It was a messy deal with lots of cooks and a pretty small kitchen. It didn't immediately conform to one of my laws for making money: do something others do not want to do.

On the other hand, for all of us it was the opportunity of a lifetime.

Value added for all the partners

SED Systems was three times the size of Calian.

It had annual sales of $22 million and had a dazzling and impressive array of space, defence and government contracts. It was also part of an exclusive club that included MDA of Vancouver, B.C., Comdev of Guelph, Ontario, and SPAR Aerospace of Toronto and Montreal that together made up most of the Canadian space industry. The Canadian government, through the Canadian Space Agency, was spending $300–500 million per year on projects like the remote sensing satellite RADARSAT and Canada's contribution to the shuttle program, the remote manipulator arm or CANADARM. SED was a partner in all of these projects and an integral part of government economic development of aerospace incentives for Canada. They also had strong management who were at that very moment telling me about the background of SED.

SED systems had a solid economic base as a result of its location in Saskatchewan. The government had a regional economic diversification program and SED was receiving the Prairie Provinces' share of government spending. The government had even set up an organization to make sure the West got their share called Western Economic Diversification (WED). As a result of this program, SED could count on a steady stream of government contracts to keep the business viable.

The problem, however, was that SED had not made money since 1965 when it was established as the Space Engineering Division (SED) of the University of Saskatchewan.

As Dugald Buchanan would describe it, "By 1990 it had been going out of business for thirty-five years." SED was first owned by a university, then by a province and subsequently had been purchased by an eastern-based aerospace company. After so many turnovers and changes of ownership and shifts of focus, it was not so surprising that SED—despite its size and assets—had failed to meet expectations.

Fleet Aerospace had bought SED in 1986 to buy their way into the space club and increase its prominence in the Canadian aerospace sector. Unfortunately, Fleet bought SED just after it won a very large defence contract called the Canadian Patrol Frigate Program (CPF). They would be building the external communications system for six new frigates at a total value of $30 million but the contract was not going well. The project was pushing SED into bankruptcy and it was pulling Fleet along with it. Fleet had been forced to pump $13 million in cash into SED to keep it alive while it struggled with this single massive contract.

In 1987, Fleet hired Dugald Buchanan to help sort out the mess. He was well-known as a tough no-nonsense program manager with a knack for making things work smoothly. At around the same time, SED had hired Ray Basler from Deloitte Touche to help them fight through the company's complex finances. The two managers were kindred spirits in every way and between them they brought order out of the chaos. It was a little late for Fleet, however, which was under significant financial stress as a result of the acquisition and a general softening of their core business: airplane frames and components. Something was going to have to change, so they put SED up for sale.

By 1990, Dugald and Ray had simplified the SED management team and had cut losing programs; for the first time SED was operating with a positive cash flow. Even so, SED was still labouring under an enormous $30 million debt. The two executives and their teams had done a wonderful job of turning the company around but the financial statements were as bad as any I had ever seen in my life. So bad that for two years SED courted suitor after suitor only to have each abandon the company at the altar. Calian, to be honest, was among the last to get an invite up the aisle.

The hurdles seemed enormous.

Buying SED would take Calian from being a small service company and place us right in the middle of the growing Canadian Technology sector. It would be our big break, and every sense in my body told me to take the risk. The space cadet in me was screaming "go for it." The street fighter in me now had to figure out how to pull off the impossible task of buying a company four times our size. We had a long to do list.

First, we had to convince the Saskatchewan government that Calian was a worthy trustee of a major provincial asset. It was not altogether clear to me if I was even in the running for the purchase of SED. I needed help and, fortunately—yet again—help was close at hand. Jim Curran had been my lawyer since the demise of Insta-Call. He was an old friend and a trusted advisor. His wife, Lisa, an interior designer, had designed my kiosk at the Ottawa International Airport in 1979! He had also assisted me with the negotiations with SAIC in 1986 and the purchase of Miller Communications in 1989.

Jim had been born and raised in Saskatchewan, and he had contacts that would prove to be very helpful. He had attended Notre Dame Private School in Wilcox, Saskatchewan, where he met Cy McDonald, a teacher, a former hockey player and a backroom strategist for Grant Devine's governing Conservative government. Jim came out to Regina with me to help with the provincial government negotiations. Eventually, he arranged a golf game with Cy MacDonald to see if we had the chemistry to work together. Cy was also on a mission to see if I was the man the government could trust to look after SED. It would be trial by golf!

By this time my father-in-law had introduced me to the skills of business golf at the cost of thousands of dollars in lost bets. Don Green was as shrewd on the golf course as he was in business. Don said you could learn more about someone on a golf course in four hours than you could doing business with him for over ten years.

Golf as a tool to know your partners

There was much information to be gleaned over four hours on the golf course. You could easily find out if the person was honest and you could also determine if they could count! You could also find out if they had a sense of humour when it was appropriate or a sense of compassion when their fellow players made a bad shot. Most important, you could discover how the player dealt with failure and how they dealt with success. That was important with a business partner because business, like golf, would always be full of ups and downs. A partner had to be able to stay calm after a good shot or bad shot. I knew that Cy would be looking at me from that perspective and I at him.

The golf game was a lot of fun. Cy was a large, good-natured man whose sense of grace and integrity was both impressive and inspiring. We liked each other and that made a good start to what would be a fun business relationship. It was the next day that Cy agreed to represent Calian with the provincial government and to show us around the legislature building to meet a few friends. He admitted it was going to be a tough sell.

The province said it would have to explore and exhaust all other options—i. e. bigger and more well-known companies—before engaging with a small technology company based—heaven forbid—in Ottawa.

To be honest, that did not upset me. I knew that the province would not have us at the top of their list. But being the favourite is not always the position of strength. The most consistent winner is the horse that runs with the pack until he turns for home and finds that extra burst of speed. The guy that is out first is often the easiest guy to beat. When you are small you don't want to concede too big a lead to your rival; the key is staying close and keeping that extra burst of energy in reserve for the finish.

Not surprisingly, one by one the other contenders either took themselves out of the running or were knocked out. This dog-and-pony show went on for two grueling years, and during that whole time SED management—Ray and Dugald mostly—suffered the indignity of being held personally responsible for the company's troubles. One chap from an American firm looked at Ray Basler during the interview process and asked him what he would be doing for a living after they bought the company. The not so subtle suggestion was that he would be the first fired after a takeover.

Smart negotiating? If that guy had done any due diligence he would have known that Ray was primarily responsible for having turned SED around—he would have and should have known what Ray's reputation in the industry was. It was egotistical short-term thinking.

Anyway, Calian finally was in a position to make its pitch.

First, Cy introduced me to Eric Berntson—the Minister of Everything. He was the Deputy Premier and Minister of Industry for Saskatchewan and, as it turned out, a fair and clear-headed executive. For weeks we had meeting after meeting in an effort to convince and then reassure Eric that the sale of Fleet would indeed be a good thing for the province. During that time I was introduced to David Tkachuck, who was in the public and government relations business and a friend of both Cy MacDonald and Eric Berntson. Between the three of them they made sure I had contact with all the right bureaucrats to hammer out a "reasonable" transaction.

They offered me a deal that met all my requirements; it was not quite as good as what they had been offering the bigger companies, however. Even so, I decided it was still solid and could work. I was ecstatic and flew home to Ottawa thinking we had a deal in the works that was good for everyone. When I got back to Ottawa I had a rude awakening. There was still one more party that needed convincing: the federal government.

Art Silverman was head of WED, and for quite some time he had been quietly monitoring the negotiations with interest. Fleet had made substantial loan guarantees that were only transferable with the federal government's approval and they did not want to do that without being invited to the negotiating table. Art was a big ex-football player and a highly competent civil servant who needed to be in the loop on this decision. I believed he felt that his nose had been put out of place with rumors that SED was going to be sold to Calian without his permission.

I kicked myself for my unforgivable shortsightedness. It had been a long process and I had allowed my enthusiasm for what appeared to be a first-place finish to blind me to a reality: what I thought was the finish line was only the third turn! We still had a long way to go!

Art had mentioned his annoyance to his next-door neighbor in Ottawa, Barry Turner. Barry, vice-president of engineering for Telesat Canada and a good friend, called me at ten that night.

"What did you do to get Art so upset?"

I gave him the Reader's Digest version of what had happened. He suggested we talk, so I drove over to Barry's house. Telesat, it turned out, had looked at SED and determined it was not the right deal for them. So Barry was up to speed on most of the key WED issues. We talked for three hours. I left Barry's house at one that morning and knew what my first call of the next day was going to be.

"Good morning Mr. Silverman," I said. "My name is Larry O'Brien of Calian Technology and I want to buy SED Systems."

He sounded a bit cool.

"I was talking to Barry Turner last night and he suggested we have a chat and I would very much like to do that."

"Were you over at Barry's last night? Did you by any chance drive a small black sports car into Barry's driveway at around ten?" His cool tone had warmed up a bit. Quite a bit, in fact.

"Yes, Sir, I was! How did you know that?" I asked.

"Well, when you sped around the corner you almost killed me and my dog!"

I was stunned. I didn't know what to say. All I could think was, crap. I've blown it!

"Yes, I do really want to see you. I want you in my office this morning." Then he hung up. I felt like I had just been summoned to the principal's office. This was not a casual invitation.

Like a dead man walking, I was heading out the door of Calian when I ran into a Terry Black, a new hire and former partner at Dy-4 Systems. Terry was a big guy who had played football for the Ottawa Rough Riders. I figured he might come in handy at my meeting with Art Silverman. I do not think I had ever been so nervous going to a meeting. Not only had I potentially screwed up a great business deal, but I had to take a bodyguard along—this was not good. I knew I had made another mistake and that made my stomach sick.

When I met Art Silverman he stared at me with menacing eyes. I thought I was finished. But then Terry bounded in behind me. Art suddenly broke into a big smile and gave Terry a big bear hug greeting. It turned out they had both played football at Ottawa University and had been friends for many years. Art had been unaware that Terry had joined Calian a few weeks before, and the meeting went ahead without a single mention of my indiscretion the previous night. WED came onside within the week and I often wondered what would have happened if I had not run into Terry on the way out of my office that day.

Was it luck? Or was it the unpremeditated consequence of having surrounded myself with outstanding talent? Truth is, I don't believe in luck. I believe in the four values approach to business. Luck is what people call success that is not earned.

We had earned our success. And it was time to celebrate.

Calian's annual New Year's Eve gala took place September 28, 1990. Calian had been celebrating our "fiscal" New Year's Eve in the same wonderful manner since 1983 and this year was special. We had booked the downtown Westin Hotel in Ottawa and there were about 250 employees, spouses, friends and guests of the company in attendance. Not only was it the main annual party for the company, it was also a way of making sure that everyone in the organization, including customers, suppliers and professionals, knew they were a special part of Calian's history and growth.

Tom Coates and I had spent the last two days in Toronto completing the biggest transaction in the company's history. Tom was a straight-laced, honest and quick-witted man whose sense of humour was legendary at Calian. I first met him in the early eighties when he was a production manager for a liquid crystal display (LCD) company by the name of Data Images. As a certified general accountant (CGA) he set up Calian's booking system in 1982 and produced our first interim statements. He joined Calian full-time in 1989 and eventually became vice president for the Services Division, running the largest part of our business.

Tom—like Ray and Dugald—had provided crucial support and leadership during the whole SED acquisition process. I could taste victory but it wasn't over yet. I had made that mistake once already and I was determined not to take anything for granted. I admit I was really nervous. The closer we came to the end the more nervous I became. There seemed to be a never-ending series of last-minute problems, but Tom and our corporate lawyer from Smith Lyons, Fred Benn, solved them all—one issue at a time.

I couldn't sleep for restlessness. This was the biggest day of my business life. I threw open the blinds of my bedroom window and nearly had a heart attack. The city was completely obscured in fog. A bank lawyer was flying in that same morning to hand over the cheque we needed to close the deal. No cheque, no deal.

"Tom," I said, "we're screwed—it's foggy! Damn! Damn! Damn! The plane will not get in! Can I phone him and get him to drive down instead of taking the plane?" I was yelling into the phone. Tom must have thought I had finally lost my marbles.

"Larry, it's only four-thirty in the morning. I think it will clear up by noon!"

"Oh, yeah. Maybe, you're right. Do you think I am being too anal?"

He was kind enough not to answer and simply suggested I go back to bed.

I had nothing to worry about. The signing and money transfer went off without a hitch and Tom and I caught a cab back to the airport for a trip home. It was gala night and we had a lot to celebrate.

The crowd at the Westin was anxious as we walked into the room. Immediately the clapping started. Slowly at first, and then one by one people stood up and Tom and I got a standing ovation. We were both embarrassed and I went to the main table and shook hands with our guests and then went straight to the microphone.

"Ladies and gentlemen, I have some good news and some bad news tonight. The good news is that this is our seventh annual New Year's Eve Party and it's our best ever!"

There was a burst of applause.

"The bad news is that there are 220 new employees at SED Systems in Saskatoon that did not have enough time to fly to Ottawa to celebrate with us!"

This single transaction increased our sales by a factor of four from $7 million for the year ending September 30, 1990 to $28. 6 million in 1991. It catapulted Calian into international satellite communications markets and into the Canadian aerospace markets in one single transaction.

Bill Casley had a wonderful expression that he often used, but it wasn't until that moment that I realized fully what it meant—how much wisdom was packed into such a simple statement. Whenever we had a contract win or a breakthrough of some sort he would smile and say, "Nothing succeeds like success!" Sustainable success was like a deep current that created its own consistent momentum. Basically, SED had been the right company with the right idea and the right people. What it had wrong was a parent company that did not have the momentum it needed to carry SED with it.

From day one, the financial results were positive for SED and Calian. Yes, the world had changed for me and Calian and it took a few months to understand how great the change. But it began with four values.

This is really important to remember: way back when I was standing by myself in the middle of the Ottawa airport flogging rented pagers to travelers who couldn't care less, I never could have imagined that within ten years I would be CEO of Calian and negotiating an acquisition of the magnitude of SED.

The lesson I want to impart is this: I said it was simple, but I never said it was easy. But there is absolutely nothing stopping you from working hard. You must work hard. It won't come easy.

Final note: it isn't about golf, but how you play the game that counts in the long run. Be consistent about you who are; don't be one kind of leader to this group of people and a different kind of leader to another. Same goes for the people you work with. Trust is the most valuable commodity you can create.

Chapter Eight

The Spark

I saved this until the end of the book for a simple reason: by now you must decide whether or not you can use the simple tools I have provided. If so, there is one more very important part of success you need to understand. If the four values are not for you, so be it. Good luck to you.

If you are still with me, there is another element of building a company that is indispensable: the spark.

I had just finished Algonquin College in the spring of 1971 and had applied for a job at Microsystems International Ltd. (MIL). MIL was Canada's only semiconductor plant and I badly wanted to work there. I knew semiconductors were the future of electronics and I had made them the focus of my collegiate efforts. MIL required all applicants to complete an exam and I was nervously waiting outside the examination room for the results.

The door sprang open and the examiner, a man named Dr. Richard Foss, congratulated me for having failed the test "the least." I knew at once that I had just been hired as a design technologist at MIL. What I didn't know was that I was about to join an industry that would change the world as we knew it.

That fall I had been working for a small band of experienced designers from Plessey Semiconductor in England. They had been lured to Canada by good salaries and the chance to work for MIL, a startup semiconductor firm owned by Northern Electric Company (NEC), which was, in turn, owned by, the safe and financially stable company, Bell Canada.

The number of things that could go wrong in the design and manufacture of a semiconductor circuit was huge; the probability of failure was inversely proportional to the size of the final component. When the circuit being designed could only be seen through a microscope it meant that any one of a million different complicating factors made the job just about impossible for anybody but the brightest and most experienced engineers. It also helped if these engineers had a strong dose of audacity and courage. Those were exactly the traits of the British engineers that came to Canada in the early seventies to build MIL. They were a swashbuckling and daring crowd in technology, business and life.

Others from MIL, me included, went off into other businesses, but none were more successful than Mike Cowpland and Terry Matthews.

The irrepressible pair met at MIL and in 1973 they founded Mitel Corporation. Mitel was soon building components that turned the pulses of a rotary dial system into modern signaling tones used in the new generation of telephone switches. Both Mike and Terry had grown up in the telephone industry, Mike with Bell Northern Research (BNR) and Terry with British Telecom. They both understood the way the telephone companies worked and to them, MIL was a gigantic playground with technology capability and a great platform from which to launch their own company.

Terry was hilariously bold and had not an ounce of shame. He had that hard-to-define quality that made you better in his presence.

Mike was a fierce competitor who could motivate by his mere presence. Bell Northern Research paid for him to go back to school and get his PhD. When he graduated he came back to work at MIL and designed telephone circuits. Mike was not your ordinary engineer; he was a consummate sports enthusiast and highly competitive tennis player who had won numerous city and provincial championships.

When they started Mitel, MIL was already showing signs of fatigue. Rumours were that staff cuts were on the horizon. They called me with an offer. We met at Mike's house for an interview that became a party that lasted until the wee hours of the morning.

I agreed to join Mitel. As the week wore on, however, I was plagued with doubts. I had worked hard to get into the semiconductor business; regardless of the potential in the telephone industry it would be—for me at least—a step down in terms of the kinds of technology issues I was passionate about. Besides, I was only twenty-four. I had a pretty good gig going with MIL. Did I really want to throw that away on a risky startup?

I notified Terry and Mike that I would not be leaving MIL after all. Thanks but no thanks.

A few days later I was on the phone with my sister Shirley. I was telling her about my decision not to join Mitel. They had been in business for about a year, I said, and they needed more technologists. They had tapped me as a guy they wanted and had really campaigned hard. They said I was nuts for sticking with a company that would be bust within a year. To be honest, as I talked to my sister I began to wonder if maybe I had blown it!

"Then what was it?" she asked. "Why do you want to stay with a company that could be out of business in a year?"

The answer was simple. "I really love what I do."

We talked some more. Suddenly the operator came onto the line. "Mr. O'Brien, I have a medical emergency call for you."

My sister's call was disconnected and there was a short pause before the operator came back onto the line.

"Okay, you can go ahead now, Dr. Matthews."

Doctor Matthews? It was Terry Matthews!

Terry had been trying to reach me—he was not happy with my decision to turn down the job at Mitel—and had grown impatient. He knew enough about how the telephone company worked to interrupt my call. Needless to say, I was white-hot angry. Who does this guy think he is!

I told him in crudely impolite terms that I would never work at Mitel. I suspect by that point he got the message. I don't regret the decision. But I learned something. I did not and do not approve of his methods, but I came to very much admire his tenacity and passion. Who did he think he was? Simple: the audacious and brilliant founder of a just-as-audacious and brilliant new technology startup. That's who!

Tenacity. Determination. Vision. Dogged relentlessness.

The spark! I said a few pages back that Terry had a hard-to-define quality that made you better in his presence. That quality was passion.

By the time I started Calian in 1982, Mitel had 5,000 employees, sales of $250 million and Terry and Mike were both multimillionaires. Their success had ignited the entrepreneurial spirit in Ottawa and for that we shall always owe Mike Cowpland and Terry Matthews an enormous debt of gratitude. Their success, first at Mitel and later with other just as successful ventures, were not coincidences. They understood their business and their market; the products they designed were products that had real value and were long term solutions to real problems their customers had. The telecommunications network evolution was predictable and inevitable: Mike and Terry understood that and acted accordingly. They were also honest, competent engineers and executives who were trying to build a business that would grow strongly and create wealth for them, their investors and their fellow employees.

The question you need to ask yourself is: am I driven to succeed like Terry and Mike?

Create a passion for success

If you do not have the passion to succeed you can develop it.

First, do not confuse a passion for success for more mundane passions.

I may say I have a passion for fast cars or single-malt scotch or pizza or whatever. That is one kind of passion, but what I am really saying is, those things are what I like to have. What I am talking about, however, is more like a state of mind. Having a passion for success is a state of mind that allows you to achieve your goals regardless of what those goals are. Passion is a statement not about what you want to have but who you are.

The good news is that anyone can develop a passion for success. The bad news is, it's a lot of hard work. Simple but not easy!

It is not news that to succeed, your passion must always be high. Intensity needs to soar over a long period, through the ups and downs of life and through the victories and defeats of your mission. You will need to work very hard for a long time to succeed. It will be tough, hard work and you will need to dig deep inside yourself for strength. This chapter will examine a few ways of developing and maintaining your passion for success.

Think of it this way: we instinctively walk across the room to pick up a book or our car keys. How come? Because we do it all the time. But look at a small child learning how to walk. It seems impossible!

What seems easy is only because we practice it every day. We forget how hard it was to learn and now we do it without thinking!

Success requires that you be passionate about your dreams and your purpose. You will need to connect your purpose with your deepest psychological needs. Having a dream that resonates with your inner needs is absolutely critical to your success. Don't worry. That is not as esoteric as it sounds. It's a question of making sure that what you want to do is matched up with the inner resources you have to get that done. Think about this: what is the difference between a dreamer and a visionary? Not much, as far as I can tell.

Except this: the visionary has the tools to make the dream come true. Right? When we want to dismiss an idea as foolish we call the person a "dreamer."

"You're dreaming! It'll never work!"

We revere, on the other hand, our visionaries. Think of the visionary as the Space Cadet with enough Street Fighter in him to brawl and fight his way to the top.

The most important choice you make on your journey to success is choosing a purpose—a mission—that will bond with your internal emotional and psychological needs. Dreaming of making a million dollars or being a rock star is not a mission. Changing a market or revolutionizing an industry is. When this happens your entire being becomes passionate because you are doing all this work for your own dream of success.

A mission cannot change; the goals and strategy can and—even must—change.

I would suggest that if you dream, you should dream big, about the goals and mission you want to achieve. The mission must be separate from specific goals and objectives. For example, if you have a choice between launching a company and making $2 million or building a company that will last forever, choose the latter. It is wise to choose a mission that is unencumbered by financial objectives.

Never let your goals become your limitations

How often have you had this experience? If only I could find a new job things would be different; things would be so much better. Then you find a new job and everything is better … at first. Then the novelty wears. Nothing really has changed and things really aren't any better. The problem is setting the bar of your goals too low and sticking with it.

A mission is a vertical aspiration; specifics like money are horizontal aspirations. The latter merely moves you from side to side but the former actually moves you forward. Now, don't get me wrong: money is not an inconsequential feature of success. The key is not making it the mission of your success. Money as a consequence of success is wonderful; money as a goal is self-defeating and ultimately pointless. Besides, we all have a basic need not only to feel valued but to do work that seems valuable. Our sense of who we are is to a large degree the sum of what we do.

Trust me, all the money in the world is poor compensation for hating what you do and not liking who you are or what you have become. We need to find our noble purpose. A noble intent. We can all identify truly noble work.

What you choose to do—either by intent or accident, nobly or ignobly, good or bad, right or wrong—will set powerful forces in motion. These forces properly harnessed can help you succeed.

What do I mean by noble intent? Does it sound a bit too highfalutin?

It isn't.

It simply means a purpose for being in business that overrides all material concerns. You know why you are in business—and you know why you want to stay in business. At least I hope you do. But why do the people who work for you want to be in business with you? Why do they want you to succeed? The answer is, they don't! Why do your customers want to continue to do business with you? Because they sympathize with your money problems and want to help you pay off that stupid mortgage on the gigantic house you can't afford?

On the other hand, if your employees and your customers see you doing something that they can believe in—if you are motivated by a purpose that motivates them or engages them as well—you have a true mission. If the only reason an employee sticks with you is the paycheque or the only reason a customer buys your product is because it is a few cents cheaper than the competitor, you don't have a mission. You don't have a noble purpose. A rival can always lower his price. An employee can easily be lured away by a larger paycheque. The right mission—the noble purpose—is the key to creating a business culture that is properly oriented to long-term growth and stability and sustainability.

But you can't fake the mission. It has to be real. It has to come from somewhere deep inside you.

Some early lessons

I was brought up in a lower middle-class environment.

We didn't have much money. We were evicted from a house and bill collectors called at all hours of the night and day. I did not feel secure as a boy. I remember my parents fighting endlessly over money and finances; I guess I came from a home that was not happy. So at a young age I came to believe that the secret to security was the accumulation of wealth.

I also had the deep and powerful need to be recognized as a success. I was a very poor student in elementary school. I failed two grades. It was humiliating and embarrassing to be treated like I was stupid—particularly because I thought I was quite bright!

It turned out I had an undiagnosed learning disability. In the fifties the science behind learning disabilities—like dyslexia—was pretty crude and as

House
Trance
Progessive

CGa

Dimitri & Like
Mike
Tomorrowland Remix.

√ ~~watch~~ watch out for this - M.Lazer
√ Clarity - Zedd
√ This is what it feels like - Armin VB
√ Thunder - WW
√ Spaceman - Hardwell
√ Lift Off - WW
Here & Now - Quintino Mashup
√ Summertime sadness -
√ Alive - Krewela
⊗ The Code/Emergency Code - WW & Ummet Ozcan.
X Center of the universe (~~Remode~~) Axwell
⊕ New world Punx - Romper
√ Mighty fools - Footracker
Animals - Martin Garix
Never Say goodbye - Dyro & Hardwell
Tuna Melt - A-track & Tommy Trash
Big Bad Wolf - ~~AB~~ Duck Sauce
The END - Tommy Trash
Reload - Tommy & Seb Ingrosso
Bingo Players - Rattle
Bingo Players - Cry (just a little) original

CANADIAN GAS ASSOCIATION – ASSOCIATION CANADIENNE DU GAZ
350 rue Sparks Street – Suite 809 – Ottawa – Ontario – K1R 7S8
TELEPHONE/TÉLÉPHONE: (613) 748-0057 – FAX/TÉLÉCOPIEUR: (613) 748-9078
www.cga.ca

Bingo Players feat Far East Movement - Get Up (Rattle)

a result I was channeled into the "slow" stream. Later, however, in high school, a province-wide aptitude test placed me in the top percentile in math and English. Better late than never! As a result, a few teachers pulled some strings and I was accepted into a college that took candidates only from the higher-level academic stream.

I was really lucky.

We all have different backgrounds. I am sure your background is different. But in many ways—the many ways I think are truly meaningful—we are all pretty much the same. I always had a skill with math and English, for instance. But no one else knew it—or believed it. Not until the test. And then everything was different.

Truth is, we all face tests of one kind or another every day of our lives. I will face a test today. So will you. How do you think you will do?

What I have come to believe is that we can never know what we can do until we come to terms with who we are. Call it self-awareness. What that does not mean is that who we think we are is the limit of what we can do! For instance, no matter how successful I may seem to someone on the outside, on the inside I will always be that embarrassed kid who failed two grades and whose family never had enough money. That is the chip on my shoulder that I grew up with, but over the years and with a lot of practice it has evolved and morphed into a mission. What could have been a negative stereotype of failure and self-defeat—I'm not smart enough—has changed into a positive concept of success—I know what I need to do. Failure as instruction, remember? I don't feel like that embarrassed kid anymore. That child is part of my biography but he is not part of my philosophy. It wasn't enough to be a success. I decided to succeed.

You need to decide to succeed.

Sounds easy! Who doesn't want to be a success? But that's the subtle but profound difference. Being a success is an abstraction. Deciding to succeed is a mindset and specific course of action: you need to figure out what your needs are—your core values—and align that exactly with your purpose. The two need to work together in a mutually reinforcing way. What follows will give you a method for increasing your self-awareness and determining the deep core values and needs that will require attention on your road to success.

We all have our baggage. Don't beat yourself up about it. What is important to focus on is, what type of baggage and how much does it weigh? Believe me when I say that it is critical to your success to know yourself and what motivates you. I am referring to the bottom-o-the-deep-well motivation.

If you can find the remote you can find your inner needs and values

Isn't it frustrating when you plonk down to watch some TV and you can't find the darn remote?

You look everywhere? Where could it have gotten too?

The passion you need to succeed is not that different from finding that remote. You need it and nothing will work without it. You know it's somewhere … but where?

After the death of Insta-Call I was bankrupt and having my wages garnished weekly. I was living with an old football buddy and licking my wounds from the devastating failure. Since my career before starting Insta-Call was in the semiconductor industry—where I had plenty of financial and emotional success—I went back to my technological roots. As we know already, I got a job at Reltek Inc., a semiconductor testing facility.

Mostly I felt safe. It was what I knew.

One day my boss, Merv, asked me to take a two-day time-management course at a local college. He wanted me to understand how to set priorities better, and I agreed. I was expecting to become a little more efficient at getting the details of the day prioritized properly. What I received instead, however, was a lesson on how to connect the dots between core values that are important to you as a person and the goals, objectives and activities that are important in your life. I had never considered what my core values were. What did I really want and why did I want it?

The purpose of the course was to provide the student with the skills to set day-to-day activity priorities. There were four stages. First we were asked to think about the values we thought were important. I never thought of this at any time in my life, so at first I struggled. The instructor prodded us with questions to help crystallize and clarify our thoughts.

Man, I was a blank! What the heck was wrong with me? Everything I came up with seemed improvised and superficial. As soon as I said it, it rang false.

Over time, however, I came to understand the nature of values. For me the values that were important were not things I had, but, rather, what I was missing in my life. It was a painful process to relive my childhood, to be honest. For so many years I had been on emotional autopilot. I realized that nothing was an accident when it came to my actions and nothing was ever quite what it seemed.

My list of values: security, recognition, health and family

The second stage of the process was to identify some big goals that would bond with the values I thought were important to me. That was a little easier: become financially secure; develop another skill that is transportable; be recognized as a success; become healthy again; marry and raise a family.

The third stage was to identify clear objectives that would help me achieve the goals I had set for myself. I also found this rather straightforward: learn the how's and why's of business success, learn to write, run 10Ks and lose weight, and find the right partner to raise a family with.

I am not sure what the ultimate value of the course turned out to be for anyone else. For me it completely changed the way I thought about my future and my life. Was it the course? No, probably not. What it did for me, however, was provide the excuse I needed but had been avoiding to seriously and thoroughly examine my life from a different perspective.

MOTIVATION CHART 1982			
Values	**Goals**	**Objectives**	**Activities**
Security	Learn about business	Build models for success	Study Merv and others Study Reltek and Insta-Cal
	Learn to write	Ottawa U	Take English 101
Recognition	Learn to write	Ottawa U	Take creative writing
Health	Lose weight	Stop drinking	Run daily
	Start running	Five 10K's	
Family	Get married	Raise a family	Get serious

For me, the most interesting aspect of this introspective view of myself is that I have reviewed my value system at least once every year for the last thirty years. There have been a few changes in goals and objectives, but the values have stood the tests of time.

The order in which they appear has changed a few times as well, but, again, the basic values have stayed constant.

Meaning what? The roots of who you are—the basic building blocks of your character—will not change much over time. Shades will occasionally appear next to what was a solid color. An appendix at the end of the book will show you how to find your inner needs and how to construct your core values. Give it a shot.

Remember:

- a mission is not a goal
- goals and strategy can change; a mission must stay the same
- before you decide what you want, figure out who you are and what you need
- a noble purpose must coincide with your inner needs
- a noble mission must be a benefit to others
- a Space Cadet creates the mission, the Street Fighter maintains it

Final Thoughts

Your Success Is Up to You

Recently I came upon some remarks by a well-known and respected financial analyst by the name of Stan Druckenmiller. In an interview with Bloomberg TV Druckenmiller was asked about how he thought the economy would perform in the years ahead.

His answer was shockingly bleak.

We are headed for a "storm," he said, that could make the financial crisis of 2008 seem like child's play.

Now, I began this book on a note of caution. By quoting Druckenmiller I do not wish to end this book on the same dire note. My intention is quite the opposite, in fact. I believe that while we all must face life with both eyes open, it is our responsibility to be optimistic even in the face of pessimism. The world will never lack for naysayers. It is much easier to admit defeat than it is to dig deep and find the resources you need to win. Not just to survive—to win.

It may or may not please you to learn that your author is a man of faith. I am a Christian. And I take my faith seriously. But it is not necessary or even very important to me whether you share my faith. What is important is that you find a value system for yourself that is consistent and true for you. I do not believe it is possible to live a meaningful life without having a structure of faith that guides our actions. We are not cogs on a giant wheel either destined or determined to a soulless fate; we are free beings who are responsible for our actions. We are architects of our fate.

71

You are the architect of your destiny.

Money can be made unethically. It happens every day. I do not believe, however, that unethical entrepreneurship is consistent with happiness.

You don't have to believe in God—or even a god. But remember what Socrates said: the unexamined life is not worth living.

What I hope this short book has done is to inspire you to examine your own life in terms of what you want and how you want to achieve whatever it is you want. Because the "how" is more important than you can ever know—far more so than the "what."

We began the book with ten principles that I followed to construct the foundation of my career as a businessman. As I said, I learned a lot over the years, and while some of the principles have been amended or added to I have never had cause to abandon them. They are as true today as they were then.

Anything else?

Well, maybe a few things.

1)   Wealth that is not shared is wealth that will not grow!
2)   Anything a person says or does or feels is about them—not you.
3)   Angry people are guilty people.
4)   Swim with the current; go with the flow—but not always.
5)   Nothing is ever what it seems; nothing is an accident and everyone is a little bit crazy.
6)   You never go broke taking a profit!
7)   What would you do if you were not afraid? And what exactly are you afraid of?
8)   The Happiest politician is a former politician
9)   It's not how hard you fall but how high you bounce.
10) Go down swinging; never let the bastards see you sweat.

Good luck!

Epilogue

In my mind there is no better way to summarize the values that created my entrepreneurial success than to describe how they failed me and fell apart in my venture into politics from 2006 to 2010. I am happy to be out of politics—all of the skills I developed over a lifetime in business were of no practical use to me in the field of politics.

Quite frankly, the differences between practical politics and ethical business are chilling and I believe the differences will have a long-term effect on both our economy and our democracy. It might even be argued that the difficulties with making the wise choices for our countries and cities may have driven the need for some of you to consider starting your own business.

I spent four years as mayor of the capital of Canada—Ottawa. During those four frustrating years I spent a lot of time and effort dissecting the differences between business and politics from the perspective of one who had just been thrown through the "looking glass." Interestingly, it is hard for me to describe the differences between the two in specifics.

But maybe this story will help. It was 2009 and I had just started making some headway in reducing costs. Not surprising, the cuts were going to result in cutbacks to services and staff and neither the union nor the city councilors were happy. As a businessman, the idea that costs could be cut without raising taxes made reducing services the only option. If there was another way, I was only too happy to hear about it. In fact, I had thought we were making progress.

Instead, the city council voted my budget down and voted to raise taxes 4. 9 percent!

I was stunned. I was embarrassed and humiliated. We were finally getting to the root of our spending problems at city hall. A few more days of hard work would have saved taxpayers tens of millions of dollars. In fact, we had already finished cutting six million dollars from our annual budget that morning!

I deeply respected Councilor Rick Chiarelli. He was one of the smartest guys I ever met and very politically savvy. And one of the most likeable. I thought he would be an excellent mayor himself one day. So I invited Rick to my office for a cup of coffee and a post mortem on what the heck had happened. I thought it only fair to get his perspective. It was a tough learning curve I was on.

The meeting was cordial enough. We sat at the round table in my office and chatted for a few minutes by way of warm up. Finally, I told Rick how stunned I was about the vote. I had thought we had been making progress. What happened?

He took it in stride. Basically, he suggested that I shouldn't take it personally. The cuts I had suggested amounted to a tough sell—too tough a sell. No councilor backing those cuts had a snowball's chance in heck of being reelected. He even suggested the vote could end up being a plus for my political career! I could blame council for not achieving my tax target.

I was thinking of the state of the budget and the long-term fiscal and social effects of the budget on the taxpayers and the city, but Rick was schooling me in political reality: what are the political implications and repercussions. I had to give my head a shake.

Rick was right, of course. At least, he was right if by right you mean doing what you need to do to survive and thrive in politics as it exists today. I realized that after the fact. Jean Chrétien once said that the number-one job in politics is getting elected and then reelected!

How different business is! A CEOs power is based on his or her ability to sustain profits. A CEO is paid to prioritize the challenges of future growth, prosperity and survival of the corporation he leads. The CEO then marshals the resources of the organization to solve these problems in order of priority. To call a CEO a problem-solver would be a simplification because in modern, complex organizations the CEO (on his/her own) could never have all the skills required to identify the myriad of solutions. Rather, the CEO accepts the ultimate responsibility of testing and then choosing from a universe of solutions recommended by the senior management team.

In a fast-paced world of growth, making the right choices is more important than ever to the survival of the organization. In business there is no committee to hide behind. The buck truly stops with the CEO. Same is true for the small business owner.

As I have outlined in this book, I have always used four principles to test the validity of business options: honesty, value, timing and prudence. From the "school of hard knocks" I learned that testing resolutions against a constant framework of sound values would enable better (and more timely) judgment and decision-making. Even more beneficial to having a common evaluation methodology is to ensure that decisions are harmonized with a constant and predictable management theme (mission).

The four-values benchmark worked in business. In politics ... not so much. And I think that is a real shame and something that needs to be addressed.

As I have said before, the business is a reflection of the businessperson. You don't stop being a father or mother or husband or wife or hockey coach or PTA member when you put on the apron or pick up the hammer or walk into the boardroom. I was not comfortable with the ethical sliding scale that was the measuring rod of choice among politicians.

Politics—at least politics as I see it being waged—is not based on values but on short-term profits. After years of training as an ethical entrepreneur I found myself in a world where I simply could not function.

If ethical entrepreneurship is to mean anything—and I think it means everything in the long run—ethics has to frame all of life. Including politics.

Stay tuned ...

Appendix

Finding Your Inner Needs: a Practical Exercise

Here's a list of common descriptors we use everyday. Run through it and tick off the ones you think most define the essence of who you are. Not who you want others to think you are—but the real you. Be honest. These are your core values. Feel free to add values you don't see on the list. (This exercise has been adapted from Steve Pavilina . com)

☐ Acceptance	☐ Affection	☐ Art
☐ Accessibility	☐ Affluence	☐ Articulacy
☐ Accomplishment	☐ Aggressiveness	☐ Artistry
☐ Accountability	☐ Agility	☐ Assertiveness
☐ Accuracy	☐ Alertness	☐ Assurance
☐ Achievement	☐ Altruism	☐ Attentiveness
☐ Acknowledgement	☐ Amazement	☐ Attractiveness
☐ Activeness	☐ Ambition	☐ Audacity
☐ Adaptability	☐ Amusement	☐ Availability
☐ Adoration	☐ Anticipation	☐ Awareness
☐ Adroitness	☐ Appreciation	☐ Awe
☐ Advancement	☐ Approachability	☐ Balance
☐ Adventure	☐ Approval	☐ Beauty

☐ Being the best	☐ Compassion	☐ Curiosity
☐ Belonging	☐ Competence	☐ Daring
☐ Benevolence	☐ Competition	☐ Decisiveness
☐ Bliss	☐ Completion	☐ Decorum
☐ Boldness	☐ Composure	☐ Deference
☐ Bravery	☐ Concentration	☐ Delight
☐ Brilliance	☐ Confidence	☐ Dependability
☐ Buoyancy	☐ Conformity	☐ Depth
☐ Calmness	☐ Congruency	☐ Desire
☐ Camaraderie	☐ Connection	☐ Determination
☐ Candor	☐ Consciousness	☐ Devotion
☐ Capability	☐ Conservation	☐ Devoutness
☐ Care	☐ Consistency	☐ Dexterity
☐ Carefulness	☐ Contentment	☐ Dignity
☐ Celebrity	☐ Continuity	☐ Diligence
☐ Certainty	☐ Contribution	☐ Direction
☐ Challenge	☐ Control	☐ Directness
☐ Change	☐ Conviction	☐ Discipline
☐ Charity	☐ Conviviality	☐ Discovery
☐ Charm	☐ Coolness	☐ Discretion
☐ Chastity	☐ Cooperation	☐ Diversity
☐ Cheerfulness	☐ Cordiality	☐ Dominance
☐ Clarity	☐ Correctness	☐ Dreaming
☐ Cleanliness	☐ Country	☐ Drive
☐ Clear-mindedness	☐ Courage	☐ Duty
☐ Cleverness	☐ Courtesy	☐ Dynamism
☐ Closeness	☐ Craftiness	☐ Eagerness
☐ Comfort	☐ Creativity	☐ Ease
☐ Commitment	☐ Credibility	☐ Economy
☐ Community	☐ Cunning	☐ Ecstasy

- [ ] Education
- [ ] Effectiveness
- [ ] Efficiency
- [ ] Elation
- [ ] Elegance
- [ ] Empathy
- [ ] Encouragement
- [ ] Endurance
- [ ] Energy
- [ ] Enjoyment
- [ ] Entertainment
- [ ] Enthusiasm
- [ ] Environmentalism
- [ ] Ethics
- [ ] Euphoria
- [ ] Excellence
- [ ] Excitement
- [ ] Exhilaration
- [ ] Expectancy
- [ ] Expediency
- [ ] Experience
- [ ] Expertise
- [ ] Exploration
- [ ] Expressiveness
- [ ] Extravagance
- [ ] Extroversion
- [ ] Exuberance
- [ ] Fairness
- [ ] Faith
- [ ] Fame

- [ ] Family
- [ ] Fascination
- [ ] Fashion
- [ ] Fearlessness
- [ ] Ferocity
- [ ] Fidelity
- [ ] Fierceness
- [ ] Financial independence
- [ ] Firmness
- [ ] Fitness
- [ ] Flexibility
- [ ] Flow
- [ ] Fluency
- [ ] Focus
- [ ] Fortitude
- [ ] Frankness
- [ ] Freedom
- [ ] Friendliness
- [ ] Friendship
- [ ] Frugality
- [ ] Fun
- [ ] Gallantry
- [ ] Generosity
- [ ] Gentility
- [ ] Giving
- [ ] Grace
- [ ] Gratitude
- [ ] Gregariousness
- [ ] Growth

- [ ] Guidance
- [ ] Happiness
- [ ] Harmony
- [ ] Health
- [ ] Heart
- [ ] Helpfulness
- [ ] Heroism
- [ ] Holiness
- [ ] Honesty
- [ ] Honor
- [ ] Hopefulness
- [ ] Hospitality
- [ ] Humility
- [ ] Humor
- [ ] Hygiene
- [ ] Imagination
- [ ] Impact
- [ ] Impartiality
- [ ] Independence
- [ ] Individuality
- [ ] Industry
- [ ] Influence
- [ ] Ingenuity
- [ ] Inquisitiveness
- [ ] Insightfulness
- [ ] Inspiration
- [ ] Integrity
- [ ] Intellect
- [ ] Intelligence
- [ ] Intensity

- [ ] Intimacy
- [ ] Intrepidness
- [ ] Introspection
- [ ] Introversion
- [ ] Intuition
- [ ] Intuitiveness
- [ ] Inventiveness
- [ ] Investing
- [ ] Involvement
- [ ] Joy
- [ ] Judiciousness
- [ ] Justice
- [ ] Keenness
- [ ] Kindness
- [ ] Knowledge
- [ ] Leadership
- [ ] Learning
- [ ] Liberation
- [ ] Liberty
- [ ] Lightness
- [ ] Liveliness
- [ ] Logic
- [ ] Longevity
- [ ] Love
- [ ] Loyalty
- [ ] Majesty
- [ ] Making a difference
- [ ] Marriage
- [ ] Mastery
- [ ] Maturity

- [ ] Meaning
- [ ] Meekness
- [ ] Mellowness
- [ ] Meticulousness
- [ ] Mindfulness
- [ ] Modesty
- [ ] Motivation
- [ ] Mysteriousness
- [ ] Nature
- [ ] Neatness
- [ ] Nerve
- [ ] Nonconformity
- [ ] Obedience
- [ ] Open-mindedness
- [ ] Openness
- [ ] Optimism
- [ ] Order
- [ ] Organization
- [ ] Originality
- [ ] Outdoors
- [ ] Outlandishness
- [ ] Outrageousness
- [ ] Partnership
- [ ] Patience
- [ ] Passion
- [ ] Peace
- [ ] Perceptiveness
- [ ] Perfection
- [ ] Perkiness
- [ ] Perseverance

- [ ] Persistence
- [ ] Persuasiveness
- [ ] Philanthropy
- [ ] Piety
- [ ] Playfulness
- [ ] Pleasantness
- [ ] Pleasure
- [ ] Poise
- [ ] Polish
- [ ] Popularity
- [ ] Potency
- [ ] Power
- [ ] Practicality
- [ ] Pragmatism
- [ ] Precision
- [ ] Preparedness
- [ ] Presence
- [ ] Pride
- [ ] Privacy
- [ ] Proactivity
- [ ] Professionalism
- [ ] Prosperity
- [ ] Prudence
- [ ] Punctuality
- [ ] Purity
- [ ] Rationality
- [ ] Realism
- [ ] Reason
- [ ] Reasonableness
- [ ] Recognition

☐ Recreation	☐ Self-respect	☐ Success
☐ Refinement	☐ Sensitivity	☐ Support
☐ Reflection	☐ Sensuality	☐ Supremacy
☐ Relaxation	☐ Serenity	☐ Surprise
☐ Reliability	☐ Service	☐ Sympathy
☐ Relief	☐ Sexiness	☐ Synergy
☐ Religiousness	☐ Sexuality	☐ Teaching
☐ Reputation	☐ Sharing	☐ Teamwork
☐ Resilience	☐ Shrewdness	☐ Temperance
☐ Resolution	☐ Significance	☐ Thankfulness
☐ Resolve	☐ Silence	☐ Thoroughness
☐ Resourcefulness	☐ Silliness	☐ Thoughtfulness
☐ Respect	☐ Simplicity	☐ Thrift
☐ Responsibility	☐ Sincerity	☐ Tidiness
☐ Rest	☐ Skillfulness	☐ Timeliness
☐ Restraint	☐ Solidarity	☐ Traditionalism
☐ Reverence	☐ Solitude	☐ Tranquility
☐ Richness	☐ Sophistication	☐ Transcendence
☐ Rigor	☐ Soundness	☐ Trust
☐ Sacredness	☐ Speed	☐ Trustworthiness
☐ Sacrifice	☐ Spirit	☐ Truth
☐ Sagacity	☐ Spirituality	☐ Understanding
☐ Saintliness	☐ Spontaneity	☐ Unflappability
☐ Sanguinity	☐ Spunk	☐ Uniqueness
☐ Satisfaction	☐ Stability	☐ Unity
☐ Science	☐ Status	☐ Usefulness
☐ Security	☐ Stealth	☐ Utility
☐ Self-control	☐ Stillness	☐ Valor
☐ Selflessness	☐ Strength	☐ Variety
☐ Self-reliance	☐ Structure	☐ Victory

☐ Vigor   ☐ Warmth   ☐ Wittiness

☐ Virtue   ☐ Watchfulness   ☐ Wonder

☐ Vision   ☐ Wealth   ☐ Worthiness

☐ Vitality   ☐ Willfulness   ☐ Youthfulness

☐ Vivacity   ☐ Willingness   ☐ Zeal

☐ Volunteering   ☐ Winning

☐ Warm-heartedness   ☐ Wisdom

Choose the top six and put them in order of importance for you as a person. Take a few days to do this, since it is critical to the outcome you are seeking. Once they are clear in your mind, choose some life or business goals that relate closely to your values. These goals need to feel right deep inside and you will know when they resonate inside your core. After that, choose some objectives that can help you prioritize your daily activities. Start by listing your core values below:

1)

2)

3)

4)

5)

6)

Then, define some goals that relate to the values, then some objectives and finally daily activities that enable you to meet your objectives. Read my 1982 values chart again and you will get the idea. It's a simple way to set your daily priorities and critical in the process of achieving your goals. Hey, I said simple not easy. There are lots of Time Management courses that take a similar approach and it may be worth taking one at your local college.

When I realized that knowing how to write was key to my financial security I went to Ottawa University and took English 101. It was hard work, but I was developing a skill set (writing) that I could take with me anywhere I went. It was a lot of work to take a course, study business and work at a day job at the same time. But each day I always found time to work on my English assignments because they tracked right back to my core values and need for security. It is very powerful to be motivated by your own values.

Remember, success is simple but not easy. It will take years of hard work, but it will be the best way to provide security for you and your loved ones.

About the author

Larry O'Brien used the last thirty-five dollars in his account to found the high-tech company Calian Technologies Ltd. in 1979. Today it is one of the most successful technology companies in Canada with annual sales of more $225 million. In 2006 Larry won a landslide election as mayor of Ottawa. He was named 1996 Business Person of the Year; was the winner of the Premier's Technology Award in 1997; and was honoured as the United Way's Person of the Year in 2006. He lives with his wife in Ottawa. Asked if he grew up in Ottawa, O'Brien answers "Not yet, but it could happen."

CPSIA information can be obtained at www.ICGtesting.com
Printed in the USA
LVOW122321010413

327057LV00003B/57/P